You Don't Know Jack!

You
Don't Know

Jack!

How Antics from My Late Husband's Spirit
Give Undeniable Evidence of Afterlife

BOBBI RISE

Spring Lake | New Jersey

Dedicated to
My Ghost Writer in Spirit

To Jack, thank you for co-creating this book with me, and for loving me past our vow "till death do us part." Thank you for working so hard to stay alive against all unbelievable odds so we could be together longer. And now, thank you for teaching me how to live and love "together" in our new normal of different frequencies... including giving me the substance of this book.

Your wonderful sense of humor lives on, too, and I am so grateful to know that. Your soul essence continues to keep things light and can bring happiness to others in the form of comfort. They will see from your efforts that our loved ones who have passed on are not gone. You are showing us all that our consciousness lives beyond the body, and love never ends.

Thank you for all your signs and messages to "open me up" and challenge my skepticism all the way. It took some work on your part to show me the energy of your Spirit is not just "out there," but always around me. I love that you keep trying to encourage me to be your voice as you communicate from the other side. Another big thank you for giving me the title for "our book." *You Don't Know Jack!* is so perfect on many levels. How wonderful it is that you can still be so smart, clever, and funny just like you were when you were here in your physical body. You have become that rare "white crow" that people don't believe exists until they see one.

And thank you for the perfect life together, two beautiful, intelligent daughters, and memories I will cherish eternally in my heart.

With Gratitude

To Gail, my medium extraordinaire, thank you so much for helping me out of my dark hole of grief with your outstanding evidential readings. Contacting you at gailandspirit@gmail.com left no doubt I was contacting Gail *and Spirit* because Jack was always around and communicating with us. Your love and support have changed my life, and I will be forever grateful!

To "Pattily," thank you always for your loving friendship and clever humor over the decades. Your opinion was so important to me because I value your wise perspective on life. You were my chapter-by-chapter cheerleader, and I love you for your big heart and your kind and gentle spirit.

To Yvonne, my dear, dear friend, who is always there for me, supporting me in my life in every way. Your insight and advice are always spot on. I love that I was your teacher and now you are mine, and that we keep changing and exchanging roles over the decades. I can't thank you enough for coaching me through this book. It truly gave me the confidence to make the book happen. Jack loves you still, and he so appreciated your editing his three books. How cool was it that he knew you could be the receiver of Gail's "spirited communication" from him? And he trusted you'd deliver it to me! Thank you from my whole heart.

To Judy and Ron who let me lean on them and ask a zillion questions to keep Jack alive for the last fifty-plus years, and even more so during all the months I was his caretaker. Jack appreciated it so much, too. And Judy, thank you for reminding me daily that you love me. Your big-sister, kind, listening ear has been so appreciated during the hardest time of my life. Because of you, I am reminded that there are angels on Earth, and you are one of them. Thank you for always being so selfless and caring to me and to absolutely everyone who knows you. Your famous chocolate chip cookies have healed more souls than I can count, and I'm sure they are one thing Jack really misses from the hereafter.

Lucie Dickenson, you have made this book possible, helping me get "our" message out there and creating such a wonderfully supportive and loving author journey for us together along the way. A big hug of appreciation to my new friend!

To all those dear friends and family who came to be by my side when Jack transitioned, bringing me food, flowers, and a kind, listening ear... you made the healing start to happen, and I couldn't be more grateful.

And to the love of my life, I do know we will be connected forever... thank you for keeping your promise to connect after passing and proving it to me. And you're right, I "don't know (the new) Jack," but I will someday... when I get there. In the meantime, I will watch and listen for your guidance, keep your memory alive, keep it light in your honor, and love you forever... I promise.

"Chance favors the prepared mind."

-Louis Pasteur

"I thoroughly enjoyed the many after death contacts that Bobbi perceived from her 'departed' husband Jack. I've studied afterlife topics for fifty years, but never read such a variety of firsthand experiences as described by Bobbi. I highly recommend "You Don't Know Jack!" for all people, especially for those grieving a beloved person or pet. Your degree of certainty that life and love continue after bodily death will certainly be heightened by reading this book."

- Mark Pitstick MA,
DC SoulProof.com SoulPhone.com

Table of Contents

Introduction

"Just write the damn book!" I heard my late husband declare right as I started to wake up one morning. I recognized his low-resonant voice in my head the same way one can mentally "hear" the memorized voices of a famous singer or a warning parent. More telling was that it was his personal style of blunt humor, which, by the way, I totally understood. I really had been seriously procrastinating from writing "our book" for months, and yet I couldn't wait to share the tons of amazing signs and messages I had been receiving from him for a little over a year since he passed. Judging by my husband's to-the-point morning wake-up call, I am sure he wanted me to share all his efforts sooner rather than later to help comfort those in grief. I actually appreciated his nudge so I would stop stalling with the expectation of more clever and humorous communications showing me he was not gone. It was time to begin.

I had been oblivious to his Spirit's efforts to connect at first, too busy grieving my fifty-four-year loss even though his passing wasn't a surprise. By age seventy-four, he had accumulated so many health conditions that had combined to be more than he could survive. Up to that point, his will to live, our unwavering efforts, and our hope seemed to have kept him going until it just couldn't anymore. His last breath from the hospital bed in our living room was on the early morning of December the twelfth, right before Christmas. At that time, paying attention to signs wasn't even a consideration because I needed to survive the immediate and required formalities. There were accounts to close, a business to end, deeds and titles and insurance forms to deal with, not to mention surviving the holidays all with the unrelenting feeling of underlying sadness and separation.

With the first few signs, like the flickering lights and questionable error messages on the thermostat, I had taken a skeptical approach, overthinking so many unexplainable events, challenging myself so as not to think I was crazy. With his constant attention-getting efforts, I finally became aware of his attempts to communicate. And after the multiple coincidences and synchronicities became glaring, I knew it was him. His efforts came in ways he promised, at relevant times, in remembered circumstances, in familiar places, or words, or wishes, and especially through his famous naughty humor. His signs and messages were varied, but regular. His strong presence and persistence, as in his physical life, became undeniable in his afterlife.

I have become so impressed and grateful that he has shown me that his loving consciousness is still around me. Because of this, I feel compelled to help any of you out there who have had significant loss to find a new perspective in your grief, too. Giving you a sampling of my husband's communications may help you to see the range of possibilities you might look for if you're so inclined. I've included those on the computer, phone, thermostat, appliances, lights, alarms, and office equipment, as well as feathers, hawks, red cardinals, moths, bees, blue herons, and even medium readings, free-writing messages, physical items moved, and more. It has been such a broad and impressive range! In fact, just knowing that our loved ones don't stop existing, but that they simply transition from their physical bodies into lighter frequencies of energy, has certainly helped me end that gut-wrenching sense of separation. It's now my gift to you. I believe that as I share my experiences of continued love, then maybe you can know that love is right there for you as well. And since my husband always so enjoyed making people laugh his entire life, I now get to be his voice to keep it light from the other side. This is our story.

Let's Have a Little Chat

Before we get started, I feel the need to describe the structure of this book. It is not chronological. I decided to group the communications from my late husband's Spirit by themes, as you will see in the Table of Contents, and not in the order that I received them. In fact, I haven't even shared all his efforts... not because they weren't worthy, but because I felt I had described enough to deliver "our" message clearly. I only chose those signs and messages that happened during the first year after my husband passed.

In addition, this is not a bibliography. I chose only relevant bits and pieces from our fifty-four years together prior to his transition. More than that would be a whole other book.

Also, for those of you who are experiencing a recent loss, my heart is with you. I will always miss my husband's physical presence and understand the serious need to process that grief. However, before starting this book, I promised myself (and Jack) I would keep it positive. With that in mind, I made a conscious decision (and a lot of effort) not to dwell on the tears and sadness. I wanted to keep the reading light, but by no means should that be seen as an effort to lessen the importance of the subject matter. After all, communicating with your loved one from the afterlife is powerfully life-changing!

Lastly, my understanding of the capabilities of our soul's energy won't be revealed to me until I cross over, so I make no claims to know about how it all works (ergo the title). At times you will notice I have even capitalized words such as Source, Universe, Light, and Love in an attempt to use them to mean that magnificent, all-powerful, and eternal state of the Divine. I feel I've witnessed the power of the energy of Love and want to share that discovery experience so you can, too!

"Concerning matter, we have been all wrong. What we have called matter is energy, whose vibration has been so lowered as to be perceptible to the senses. Matter is spirit reduced to a point of visibility. There is no matter."

-Albert Einstein

Chapter 1 – Technical Antics

*M*y husband was a funny guy... confident, clear about right and wrong, a man's man, and deeply loving and spiritual underneath that tough exterior. He was always the first to volunteer or give someone the shirt off his back whenever he saw the need. He held steadfast to his own principles to keep high standards, while embracing all others for being and doing the best they could. I always enjoyed our conversations, too, especially about our beliefs. We certainly had many discussions in our fifty-four years together about what we thought happened when we died. He said he'd probably go first, so he'd "let me know when he got there," promising some signs to let me know if we could still connect. He said he'd probably "mess with the thermostat" somehow, but I'd have to wait and see.

His many years in Catholic school followed by a course on Great Religions of the World in college led him to a simple belief about "the beyond." His thinking became more global with a new awareness of the origins, doctrines, and holy books for each major religion. He concluded that the basic, soul-level essence of his energy would "continue on" into the afterlife, and his Heaven or

Hell would depend on the memory he'd take with him of how he treated others and the planet while here on Earth. What he caused others in comfort, love, or pain would surely be made clear on the "other side," and he would then rejoice or suffer accordingly in his eternal consciousness. I liked his thinking and began to open my own mind into a broader and more spiritual direction as well. He was interesting, comfortable in his own skin, and didn't take himself too seriously. He could change channels from our deep discussions to being silly with the little grandchildren, and then back to an emergency job-related troubleshooting call without blinking an eye. He knew how to settle my worries, and I learned a lot from him.

Keeping it light and being fun was his delivery style. He made people laugh wherever he'd go to raise the energy in the room, and it worked. His nephews always asked to be seated at Uncle Jack's table at weddings knowing he'd do something naughty to surprise them like flick a sugar packet at one of them and whisper, "Food fight!" He was their six-foot-three, 220-pound partner in crime. Students in his HVAC (heating, ventilating, and air conditioning) technical training seminars wrote great reviews about how he could take dry, technical lessons and make them come to life with colorful, edgy humor. The president of one of his professional groups still tells the story of the night he called our house and asked to talk with him. I didn't know who it was but offered to take a message, and the man's voice answered with, "Are you Lucky?" I was shocked and a little concerned about this strange caller. He asked again, "Are you Lucky?" After he explained who he was, and that Jack had put "Lucky" down as his wife's name on the member spreadsheet, I gave him my real name. We both laughed. He said, "Why am I not surprised!"

Friends and neighbors also knew to expect the unexpected with him, and his golf buddies to this day still swap funny stories of his rascally behavior. His wit was quick but tempered enough to measure boundaries so as not to offend anyone. Everyone always laughed at how he got away with saying what he did. He had a strong intuitive sense for people's ability and desire to be playful, and his friends enjoyed the guaranteed opportunity to spar with him. His office phone would ring, and Jack would always check caller ID to make sure he could bust with the caller.

He'd answer, "Yo mamma!" or adopt the Anthony Soprano North Jersey accent, "What do you want? I'm busy!" During his last few months, his heart wasn't strong enough to return the blood back to his head when he stood up. It was called orthostatic hypotension, and he was unable to even get up out of his bed without passing out. In spite of this, he kept his sense of humor right to the end. When the home health aide would come through the front door in the morning while I was helping him get dressed, he'd call out, "Help, elder abuse!" She would always laugh and say, "I'm sure you deserve it!"

He did love to shock people with his comedic naughty routine, too. About a year before he passed, he was in the hospital with congestive heart failure, and his cardiologist was doing rounds. She came into his room with another doctor and said, "Jack, I'd like you to meet my friend, Dr. So-and-So." Jack immediately smiled and responded, "You have friends?" His doctors truly enjoyed his sense of humor, and many made phone calls to me after his passing and shared that with me. And I remember one time, years ago, we were walking through Home Depot when a sales guy asked him if he needed help. Jack asked, "Where are your shovels? I need to bury my wife under the maple tree in the back yard." Another time Jack was waiting for me outside of an apartment building of a vacationing friend for whom I was cat-sitting. Her downstairs neighbor had called the police because he heard footsteps in the apartment above and was worried someone had broken into her apartment. The policeman arrived just as I finished putting down the cat food and came outside to lock the door. He walked up to Jack, who had been sitting on a patio bench waiting for me, and he asked him if he could identify me. Jack said, "I've never seen this woman before in my life." I snapped, "Jack!" and swatted him on the arm. Jack laughed and then the officer laughed. He was still smiling as I explained why I was there.

He knew this guy was really going to get an earful from "the wife" on his way home.

I also want to be honest here, it wasn't always hunky dory. We certainly had our arguments, stresses, and differing opinions as all couples do. But, buried deep under it all was the love we shared, so we learned how to be more objective and to see the bigger picture. And fortunately, or unfortunately, his health conditions always made us confront a dim reality, a cloud over our heads, that we didn't have forever. When he first was diagnosed with type 1 diabetes at age twenty-two, it was in the early 1970s. Back then the medical prognosis was not good. The predicted damage to his body from lack of blood sugar control threatened to shorten his life and cause serious complications like blindness, kidney problems, and loss of feet or legs. It truly made us cherish our time together more than most people who don't experience that clock ticking. We had to let the small stuff go because we could see most differences were relatively just that... small stuff. In addition, we both understood the roles our souls would play during this physical time together... each taking turns at teacher, student, caregiver, nurturer, protector, and more. They say there's nothing like a spouse to teach you the lessons you need to learn about yourself and help you grow. Looking back, we certainly had our share of growth!

****

Now Jack and I had been brought up to believe that loved ones that pass on might be watching over us like guardian angels, or they might be able to support us somehow. My grandmother used to tell me to pray for guidance or ask our (deceased) great-grandparents for help. Jack's mom spoke of special, spiritual relatives that had strong intuition and shared what they sensed with surprising accuracy.

Throughout our five decades together, our spiritual interests expanded. We had medium readings with undeniable evidence coming through. We loyally watched *Crossing Over with John Edward* on television every Friday night for several years. These shows blew our minds with information John Edward would "bring through" that only the recipient of the reading could have known.

One man had gone into the laundry room of his home, held his transitioned son's shirt to smell his smell and sobbed. He told no one. John Edward described that private moment perfectly, including a description of the room in the house and the shirt. Another participant of the show had her deceased mother come though. The mother thanked her daughter for what she whispered into her ear while in a coma before she passed. John Edward gave the exact words, "It's okay to go, Mom. I'll be fine. I love you." The daughter was floored as she acknowledged it was exactly what she said. She explained that she and her mom were alone in her hospital room, and shortly thereafter, the mom took her last breath. And one episode in particular was the most convincing because it was a reading for Jack's aunt and cousins after his uncle had passed. The family actually went to the studio in New York City. On the day of the airing, we watched John Edward start the readings with them, sharing unknown facts about his late uncle's last days. He also spoke about the Spirits of Jack's other deceased family members, who his uncle was now spending time with. Every single quote, event, or person was validated by his family.

Through the years, we learned more and more about energy work and gradually became Reiki Masters. We took classes in Qigong and Tai Chi and learned to meditate to "feel the connection" with our loved ones on the other side. At times, we each would quietly "talk" to our grandparents who had passed hoping they would know and feel the love. In fact, one time, about a week after Jack's father suddenly had a heart attack and died, Jack asked him for a sign. That evening, both outdoor garage lights flashed as we pulled up in the driveway. Then they both went out completely. Jack figured there might be a circuit problem and would check the electric panel.

After bringing in some items from the car, he noticed both lights were back on. Then, after we put things away, we settled in to watch television, but the cable box was blinking for no apparent reason. The power on the box itself then went off for maybe only five minutes, and then suddenly clicked on and went back to normal. We were definitely startled. After it stayed on for a while, I laughed with Jack. "You asked Dad for a sign, and he gave you two!" Not long after that incident, Jack told his uncle Walt about hearing from his dad. Uncle Walt wasn't surprised. He chuckled and said, "I would have never doubted it. Your dad was always good with electricity." It was then that Jack made a deal with Uncle Walt... that whoever passed first would give a sign to the other guy to connect—not that it was a contest. His uncle had a great sense of humor, too, and they both promised to make it funny. Much to our surprise, one day several years later, the old joke fart machine in the bathroom cabinet suddenly went off. Jack and I were so shocked to hear it—forgetting it was even there. It turned out that was the day that Uncle Walt passed away. What cemented our certainty that it was a sign from him was that the little gadget was missing its batteries.

More and more, our faith in communication from the afterlife was solidified after that. We knew science had determined that we are made of quantum energy which could neither be created nor destroyed. Jack read some works of Albert Einstein and learned about frequencies. He therefore figured that only the *frequency* of our energy changes when you leave the body's density. He continued to hope he might be able to affect things electrically or electronically after he crossed over from his physical form into a purely energetic form. Since he had written three technical books, including one on electricity, and was a technical trainer for the HVAC industry, he reminded me about his promise to mess with at least our thermostat to get my attention after he passed. I remember asking him to just make sure he doesn't turn off the heat or air conditioning by mistake. He grinned and said, "I'll do my best."

What I wasn't expecting was that when he did cross over, his sense of humor could be part of his continued essence, and that he would become playful from the other side. In fact, because I was so buried in grief, anytime something failed to work or appeared to need attention, I assumed the worst until it would work fine. The initial thermostat failures, my unexplained phone notification *ding*s with no one there, lights flickering, strange electronic events, or temporary electrical failures were each perceived as a problem for me to resolve. The heavy weight of responsibilities made me focus on that. I already had piles of paperwork, a business to close, companies to inform, automatic charges to cancel, and people to notify. It took a little while before I even remembered his promise to me about the thermostat. But once I made that connection, it was clear. Although I remained somewhat skeptical when things went wrong at first, I became more and more open to the possibility that it might be him energetically tinkering with these items in the house. I guess I was just slow, or in denial, or just so sad that I didn't, or couldn't, get it quickly. In fact, unfortunately, I still kept calling for servicemen to come out and check those items over those first few months to "fix" things that had problems. I had to hear from the phone company, the cable guy, the pool vacuum repair company, the AC guy, the electrician, the Geek Squad, and the security alarm people that what they came to fix was suddenly working just fine and they couldn't explain it. I guess I needed all that validation to convince myself I wasn't just wanting it to be him. I now enjoy telling people my progression from not paying any attention to possible signs, to now saying hi to Jack or blaming him for anything mysterious that happens.

****

For example, going back to the first night after Jack passed, I heard his office phone ring and go to voicemail. I knew that he only used that phone to receive calls from people in the industry who were up against an urgent situation and wanted troubleshooting help from him. Time was of the essence for them, and I didn't want them waiting for a response that wasn't going to come. I went to play the message back to get a number to call and let them know he passed, but the voicemail had not recorded it. In fact, for the next few days, I could see the machine indicated the number of calls that came in, but none were recorded. I felt terrible thinking people might still be waiting for a return call from him. I finally called the phone company, but they couldn't explain it much less fix it. After I hung up, I discovered the fax machine was also not working as I stood waiting for an important document from the funeral home. I decided, rather than have people with an emergency wait for his call and be disappointed that he wasn't responding, I would just cancel that business phone and fax line completely. And as I did that, I happened to notice the battery-run clock on the wall had stopped at 3:44... a significant time.

There had been a loud boom that woke both of us up the night before he passed. After making sure all was okay, we both said, "goodnight, I love you," one last time. As I got into bed, I looked at the clock and it was 3:44. When I later thought about all the unusual events of those first days after his crossing, it just seemed too coincidental. And as I went to put in a new battery for the wall clock, I saw that the clock was running because the battery was fine. A year-and-a-half later and that clock is still running, so far. That just added another unexplainable piece to make me suspect that he had to have been a part of all that.

****

At the end of the same week that I was dealing with his office phone, fax, and clock not working, another group of hard-to-explain occurrences took place that made me pay even more attention. It was only one week after Jack passed. I was so absorbed in the gripping waves of grief as well as having to focus on the triaged to-do list such as still notifying everyone, planning arrangements, writing the obituary, and closing his business that I could not have made the connection between the electrical antics starting up. As I was about to go to bed, I went to lower the temperature on the thermostat for a better night's sleep and to get ahead of what was to be a hot day to follow. I noticed a warning message on the LCD screen about needing service immediately. It worried me because it would not go away no matter what I pressed. It was strange since we had just had our annual service just a few months before, and that control program was preset to remind us for our next service at the one-year mark. I couldn't adjust the temperature, but the system was still working so I gave up and went to bed.

The next morning the error message was gone, but came back the next night and, once again, disappeared when I got up again. After the third day of these unexplained "hide and seek" messages, I was tired of worrying about it and knew I needed to call the air conditioning company before it failed altogether and left me without. When I called them, I spoke to their technical service guy. After he listened to me describe what was happening, he told me what I was describing didn't make sense. He suggested that since it was fine and running normally at that moment, to call back if it happened again. The message no longer displayed or hijacked the settings, so there was no need for service that next day. I admit I still felt unsettled with the lack of an explanation as to why it was acting up, but it still didn't occur to me it could be Jack messing with it.

Fast forward to two weeks later, the thermostat was dark when I woke up in the morning, and it didn't respond with heat or cooling no matter what I did. I called for service and our long-time serviceman, Ernie, was there within an hour. After he did his troubleshooting, I heard him mumble, "Now that's the queerest thing I've ever seen." He had opened it up, seen that it had power, checked the whole system, and had no explanation for why it stopped working. It was then working fine. As I signed his work order, I saw "no charge," and under his notes for the diagnosis he had put two question marks. As he left, he said, "I am so sorry I couldn't figure out what has happened. I just can't explain it." It was at that point, and I'm not sure why, that I remembered Jack's promise to try to impact our thermostat, and suddenly my skeptical mind opened up to the possibility that he was the culprit. I didn't want to tell Ernie that I was finally figuring it out myself.

I must admit, it was the third thermostat challenge that finally did it! Jack's hat trick! This time, the thermostat really acted up, but right in front of my eyes and interactively. As the house was getting too warm that morning, I set the temperature for the air conditioning, but before I even walked away, I saw the setting jump two degrees lower. It changed right in front of my eyes! It happened a second time, but after the third time, I laughed right out loud acknowledging him and feeling thrilled by it all. There was no doubt Jack was playing with me... and it was *so him*! I actually got chills. I called my daughters and shared my excitement with them, and neither was surprised. What increased the meaningfulness was that he always used to move the setting up a couple of degrees, and I had always moved it lower. The old temperature tug-of-war game we used to play convinced me even more, and I couldn't stop grinning. I was convinced... this one was *really* him! And that was when my skepticism about the other questionable happenings began to dissolve. He was there, or at least his Spirit was. He was not gone after all! I felt a sudden rush of comfort, safety, and total joy pour over me, and then the emotions overwhelmed me into tears... very, very good tears.

****

Since that day, Jack's promise to "play around" with the electrical and electronic devices has been his primary call sign. I have (mostly) learned to pay attention and appreciate his efforts instead of immediately getting all upset, but I wasn't always paying attention. About a week after the third thermostat problem, Jack made himself known again, but this time in the kitchen. I had put a big bag of frozen vegetables in a large roasting pan, turned on the oven, and then walked away to get busy with other errands. After a while, I was back in the kitchen and noticed the "oven on" light was now off. I opened the oven door and no heat hit my face. In fact, I could touch the cold vegetables, so it had never heated up. Thinking I didn't hit the start button, I went through the process again and made sure I double-checked each step. I then repeated setting up the stove and timer, but didn't wait as long, and, sure enough, the oven turned right back off.

This was twice the oven failed. I started wondering if my oven needed repair, or worse, if it needed to be replaced. Before Jack passed, he had encouraged me to get a new stove with a convection oven, but I had hoped ours would last till the supply chain shortage would make appliances more available. I stood there and tried one more time. I waited while just hovering over the stove through the first ten minutes or so, and the light stayed on, the oven got hot, and it was suddenly working! Feeling relieved, I reset the timer and walked away.

An hour or so later, after having been totally absorbed by an insurance problem, I suddenly realized there was a strong smell of those roasted vegetables permeating the house. I quickly went back to the stove and saw that this time it was the timer that malfunctioned! The stove was now fine, but the shriveled-up veggies had completely over-roasted because no beeping went off to let me know they were done. I took the vegetables out and decided I'd better check it all now. I tested everything to see if it all did what it was supposed to, and all was fine every time. Once again, I was dealing with what appeared to be a coincidental and unexplainable set of events.

Fast forward one year... neither the stove nor the timer have ever failed again. And by the way, Jack hated to eat his vegetables! I had to laugh at what possible message he was sending by playing around with the stove, and whatever it was, I was just so happy to think he was "there" with me.

****

Once I discovered he was actually interacting with me, I had to catch myself when I would cry over him being gone. Yes, physically, he was not there to hug, talk to, and share my day-to-day life... but not gone. I had missed him so much that I didn't want to go on without him initially. Don't get me wrong, I wasn't planning to end my life, but my all-encompassing grief sapped me of the energy to want to even get out of bed in the morning. My stomach hurt and my eyes burned from all the sobbing. However, after just a month or so after he passed with all the indications started, it became clear that he had only transitioned and was not separate from me. It made life start to become more bearable. I feel so lucky that he continued to reach out by giving me countless unexplainable happenings that grabbed my attention. And his signs were very believable because they carried weight with the meaning they held between us. I give just a few more to share his ability, creativity, and the range of possibilities.

****

The very next morning after the stove mystery, I went to press the toaster handle down on the toaster, but it bounced right back up, unable to work. I checked to make sure it was plugged in, and then noticed I couldn't turn the coffee pot on either. Since they were both using the same outlet, I checked for power there and saw the ground fault button had popped. So, it was the outlet, not the toaster or coffee pot. I reset the button, and all was good. I started thinking about how this outlet was working just fine the day before when I had coffee in the afternoon. I hadn't used the toaster or coffee pot since, and nothing else was using that outlet or along that circuit, so, logically, how could that have even happened? Once again, no known explanation made me start blaming Jack, which I admit I began to enjoy. Afterall, nothing bad was really happening, no costs, and nothing was broken. He was just getting my attention... and I was totally embracing it now. In fact, at times when I would break down missing him, I would actually ask him to keep showing me he was around.

Another event that appeared to be more like Jack's doing (but you decide!) was the time the control on the refrigerator door that shows which ice machine choice is currently selected changed lights. I always left it on the ice cube selection—not crushed ice, not water, and not the light. I went to get some ice cubes, and when the glass pushed against the lever, water came out. As I changed the selection back to ice cubes, the light for crushed ice lit up, changing my selection by itself. At this point, I could just imagine him cracking up right then. He had certainly worked very hard trying to get my attention with the oven, the timer, the toaster, the outlet, and now the refrigerator ice machine. I had to give him credit for his efforts! And just so you know, the outlet and the ice machine selector on the refrigerator door have been fine ever since!

My last example was with my car and had considerable meaning behind it. Since I have been in two major accidents totaling my cars, I am not a brave driver. Going to new places at a distance would also raise my anxiety. He always volunteered to drive me whenever he could, or he would at least take me out on dry runs in advance of my appointments so I could get the lay of the land beforehand. It's something I miss so much and have asked him to let me know he's now my support Spirit watching over me. On this day, I had just picked up a friend to go to lunch, and I noticed it seemed loud in the car. I realized the sunroof was wide open, and I hadn't opened it. In fact, I had never opened it before, and I didn't even know where the sunroof button was. My friend and I were laughing as I pulled over. We both looked all over for the button and finally found it between the visors. My friend knew Jack very well and immediately declared it was him up to no good. The sunroof has never mysteriously opened again, and she stills tells her "Jack story."

****

One of the hardest realities of losing my lifelong partner was my inability to share... share time together, share emotions, stories, opinions, decisions, etc. That left me feeling miserably lost at first. But one of the most comforting aspects of my discovering that Jack's Spirit, or essence, or consciousness was still around me was that I began to realize I was not alone. Now I know I can talk to him mentally or even out loud, and I can feel his presence with me. I know Jack is watching me, and that there's no judgement, no competition or conflict from his ego... only love. I get so excited that the powerful bond between us, our unusual openness to the energy continuum, and the "deal" we made before he transitioned have set us up for communicating.

And now that I am blessed to have this awareness, I feel the need to share that with anyone who worries about or fears a disconnection from a loved one. I know I feel less fear about dying now. I feel less alone. I feel like our love energy will always be connected even in different dimensions. The problem is, I'm learning how foreign this concept is to people who haven't given this possibility much thought. I really don't wish for others to consider me crazy, so I started recording some of my wildest and most unexplainable signs and messages. They are now documented so I can share them with others. It's fun to have proof! Stick with me. There's so much more!

"One thing I have learned in a long life: that all our science, measured against reality, is primitive and childlike. We still do not know one-thousandth of one percent of what nature has revealed to us.

It is entirely possible that behind the perception of our senses, worlds are hidden of which we are unaware."

-Albert Einstein

Chapter 2 –
Caught on Camera

I was listening to a fascinating YouTube video with Dr. Gary Schwartz speaking about his afterlife experiments at the University of Arizona. I was so impressed by how respected he is as a scientist, educated at Harvard, taught at Yale, and with five professorships: surgery, medicine, psychology, psychiatry, and neurology (definitely an overachiever). He and his team are backed by an organization that helps with the funding for his much-needed, highly sensitive equipment to detect energy frequencies for his SoulPhone Project. He said he was doing the work for those in Spirit on the other side who make the effort to let us know they are not gone. As for those people who have a hard time believing in this possibility, he compared it to the concept of the existence of the white crow: it's unbelievable until you've seen one. At that point in the video, my smartphone *dinged* with a text notification. I put YouTube on pause to see who was trying to reach me, but there was no one there. It seemed strange, but I didn't connect the specific content with the timing of that phone sound right away. I just went back to his talk and continued listening intently to the promising results of the current research.

I was so fascinated by the quality of his rigorous studies, the ability to replicate communications, the pure isolation of variables, and the triple-blind, statistically verified results showing a ninety-nine percent certainty of communication from the other side.

As I neared the end of the talk, Dr. Schwartz once again spoke of the efforts of those trying to reach us from the other side, and my phone did it again. Another notification *ding* with no message. Both times it was right when Dr. Schwartz was speaking about Spirit coming through... the white crow, if you will. That caught my attention and gave me the chills because of the repeated coincidence. I had to wonder, was it Jack? My chest filled with excitement. Was he trying to tell me he's been reaching out to me like a white crow, and I needed to pay more attention? I continued listening because now I was truly engaged and intrigued!

When the talk was over, I couldn't google Dr. Schwartz's name fast enough to read more about his credentials. As I was trying to take in all this amazing background of education, a big, red, oval-shaped blob suddenly appeared over the biography covering a part of what I was reading. It also covered some of the menu bar as well, indicating it wasn't part of the Wikipedia site. The blob was actually pulsating! That really grabbed my attention because I immediately thought that something was wrong with my laptop, as usual. Imagine sitting in front of your computer and a big, red, oval-shaped blob appears on your screen on top of what you're reading and is spread out over the menu bar! It felt supernatural (and I date myself) like *The Twilight Zone*! I grabbed my phone and recorded the oval pulsating so I could eventually show it to the Geek Squad computer repair people. I was imagining trying to describe this to them and visualizing them not believing me without seeing it for themselves.

I instantly shut down my computer hoping to stop a possible virus... just in case it wasn't Jack. Later, because I was so curious, I booted it back up and went back to that website to retrace my steps, but there was no pulsating oval. I have repeated this process several times since then, and I have never been able to reproduce it. Putting these three attention-grabbing "happenings" together felt like putting together clues to a mystery. The synchronicity was becoming clear because of the impact on both the phone and the computer with precise timing and quite a bit of creativity. To give me an attention-getting *ding* during the description of our loved ones trying to reach us was perfectly timed. Then the timing was on the money again when Dr. Schwartz compared these messages from the other side to the hard-to-believe white crow. Two references... two *dings*... followed by that big, red, pulsating shape. In the end, it was all three signs put together that created the synchronicity of Jack's message. It was very clear that he wasn't gone, but that he was right there and trying to send me a message. I got so excited that I wrote a letter to Dr. Gary Schwartz telling him about the *dings* and the red pulsating blob. I suggested that my husband's Spirit might have been volunteering to help with his research. As I wrote, I mentally asked Jack if he'd like that... if he had the time. I imagined him saying, or mentally heard back, "I have eternity."

I've since shared my video with many people whose immediate reaction was that it looked like a heart beating. One woman wondered if there might have been a glitch in that search engine software that may have caused it by error. I told her that to me it was becoming apparent that the timing was what really mattered. The only time the red oval appeared to me was in conjunction with the two unexplainable *dings*, exactly when the two white crow references were made. All three happenings certainly grabbed my attention for a reason. It wasn't so much the possibility of a red oval happening, but it was the synchronicity of how and when and under what circumstance that they all happened together. It was then that I decided to start reading about how to stay more open to signs with healthy skepticism. Once that intention was set, so much more was soon to find me.

****

Feeling more aware of possibilities now, but not wanting to ever jump to conclusions about Jack being present without evidence, I began to pay more attention to unusual or unexplained events, especially if they came in clumps or in curious combinations or with meaningful timing. Most initial signs had presented themselves as problems, or at least that's how I perceived them. Naturally they would catch my attention because I tend to fix anything broken as soon as I can. So, to reframe my thinking from something *being wrong* to see it as a possible sign would require some time to pass... it was a process to reach that conclusion. The "problem" would often prove to not be a problem as the issue would correct itself and go back to normal. Then, with that new information, I could now get new or clearer insight because I could add up all the surrounding circumstances and recognize the event as hard to explain any other way. With a little distance, I had more clarity. I grew to notice more of the context for the unusual happenings afterwards which would make it suddenly click and give me that wonderfully joyful *aha* moment.

I recognized another reason why signs aren't so immediately apparent. They can be very subtle and stretch out in steps over a span of days. Looking back, I wonder what subtle signs Jack may have tried to send me that I may have missed. As desperate as I was to have him back, I would have given anything to know he was with me right after he passed. I could have been so comforted, but my head was in a cloud just pushing through my days feeling engulfed in sadness and having to step up to solve everything coming at me. I am so grateful he was persistent on one of his messages until I finally put two and two together to get five with Jack's Feather Caper, which happened about seven months after he passed.

It was a series of events that took over a week before it hit me that it must be him and his sense of humor. I went outside very early to put out a card for the postal delivery woman to pick up on the Thursday before the July 4th weekend. As I left my front door, I could see a beautiful, pure white feather stuck in the ground, standing up like a dart under the mailbox. It was elegant. I brought it inside to save and even measured it, discovering it to be over a foot long. The next day, Friday, when I went to get the mail, there was another all-white feather in the ground, not quite as big, but also directly under the mailbox. I took it inside as well, but first gave a quick scan of my yard and my neighbors' yards to see if there were any more feathers anywhere. It was the only feather. That afternoon, I went for my walk in the neighborhood keeping an eye out for any feathers and saw none. I was feeling rather lucky for the two I found, and just a little surprised they were in the same place. On Saturday, July 2nd, when I went out to get the mail, yet another single white feather was lying in the same place on the ground as the first two, with no others in sight or in the neighborhood when I went for my walk. I took that third one inside as well, but only now did I really start thinking about how unusual this was. Three made me suspicious, so I checked the outdoor front camera for all three days, but no one had been there. I thought, "What are the odds of a single white feather, three days in a row, to be placed so noticeably right where I was sure to go every day?"

On Sunday, July 3rd, I went outside for my walk, and there was not one feather under my mailbox or anywhere else along my path. I just decided that my three-feather coincidence was over. On Monday, July 4th, a postal holiday, there was no feather in that spot again. I laughed to myself, "Of course. It's making sense now... no mail, no feather!" Could our loved ones really know these things on the other side? Like postal holidays? And what can we really know anyway? And sure enough, on Tuesday there was one single white feather right under the mailbox! I had four beautiful white feathers right where I would go and only on the days I would go there. From that day forth, there has never been another white feather anywhere in that area. After four, I realized how clever Jack had to be to cause them to be there, to stand out, and to be directly in my path to grab my attention (however his energy could do that). But that wasn't all he did with my white feathers. Wait till you hear what else happened. Late one evening, I laid out some paperwork I wanted to attend to the next day. With them, I placed all four beautiful, white feathers on the kitchen counter to remind me to take a picture of them the next morning in the right daylight. Ever since I was lucky enough to capture a video of the pulsating blob, I was really into documenting every unexplainable sign. I also started to write them down in my journal every day so I wouldn't forget any of them. I then checked that the doors were all locked, set the alarm, and went into my bedroom. The next morning, when I woke up and came out of the bedroom to turn off the alarm, I quickly saw that there were only two feathers on the counter. My brain buzzed, "No, no, no, no I'm not going crazy... and I don't sleepwalk. Where could those other two be? And they were the two biggest ones!" I knew I couldn't have blown them off as I passed by them the night before because I hadn't passed near enough to the counter to create a breeze. I looked around the area and noticed the two biggest feathers on the floor below. I picked them up, looked around, and tried to imagine any scenario that would make just those two go off the counter. I checked the air from the air ducts and stood right where the feathers were lying on the counter. I wanted to feel if there was any air flow there. I even put all four feathers back exactly as I had placed them that night before, and I left them there for five days to see what could have blown them off. They never moved an inch, not one feather, and the cooling system was going on and off, running most of that time.

Towards the end of that week, I was sharing my stories with different relatives about the appliances acting up, the pulsating oval, the unexplainable phone sounds, and the mysterious mailbox feathers. One of them laughed and suggested they were like that volleyball, Wilson, from the movie *Cast Away* with Tom Hanks... representing company to comfort me. I got his message, laughed, and became even more determined to document. He reminded me about our closed-circuit cameras that perhaps had recorded everything in that room. Once I started to review the recording, I could see the four feathers were clearly in view of the camera. I watched the recording as it played, starting from where I could see me move through the house to lock up and go to bed. I slowed the fast forward way down and patiently watched the low-light recording as the time indicator moved slowly forward and into the night. Then it happened. Suddenly, two of the feathers appeared to have flipped up into the air and settled onto the floor below like someone blew a puff of air at them. It took place after midnight, while I was fast asleep in the bedroom. There was no one else in the house, no event, no wind, nothing causing the two biggest feathers to simply flip up and fly off the counter. Once again, no explanation. I replayed it many times, and eventually, just to document this next anomaly, I made a video on my phone of that recorded playback.

Everyone I've shown this recording to has asked me so many questions about the circumstances or the air ducts, all trying to find an explanation, and none of us can make it make sense or google it away. It happened, and I believe now that if I put all elements of this feather week together—the daily mailbox feather (except for, or especially because of, the non-mail days) as well as the ones blown off the counter—it all speaks so loudly of his personality. I could just picture him smiling as he came up with this feather-blowing surprise that I wouldn't be able to explain away to know it was him. After all, I imagine him watching me process everything, feather by feather, with skepticism at every juncture, until I reached the end of all my and everyone else's possibilities. It was then that I found it easy to see it all in its full synchronicity as being Jack's humorous and persistent attempts to get my attention. I almost felt bad for him that he had to work so hard to convince me, but I was so glad he did.

****

Shortly after Jack's Feather Caper, I was beginning to write a blog post about it, and my computer screen broke out into a full crazy jiggle, the whole screen shaking so fast, back and forth. I was unable to stop it for several minutes, and I couldn't read anything. At first, it worried me that something was wrong with my computer. I quickly recorded it on my cellphone's video camera just to prove, one more time, that I wasn't making this stuff up. I clicked off the screen I was on, then went back in, and it did not happen again. Of course, I googled to find out what it could have been, and it said that a jiggling screen can happen if a driver has gone bad. However, the jiggling then stopped altogether. My computer was suddenly normal... no jiggling at all. It didn't make sense that it seemed to have fixed itself, so I didn't take my computer in for repair. I decided to wait. I learned that I needed to be patient enough to wait and see if there really was a problem, or if it was just Jack. Maybe he was trying to let me know he was still there as I was about to tell our feather story.

The following week I had arranged a Zoom meeting with Gail, the medium, who was scheduled to do a reading for me. I was so excited to possibly hear from Jack and was getting ready when I discovered my computer said it had no Wi-Fi connection. Then I grabbed Jack's computer, but the same error message came up. Everything else that relied on our Wi-Fi connection in the house was working fine. I started thinking it might be my own excitable energy affecting something, as my husband used to claim when I had problems that he didn't have. I took some deep breaths, relaxed into my chair, and quickly downloaded the app on my phone to make the meeting. As soon as Gail came into view on my little phone screen, she shared that she was having trouble getting connected to Wi-Fi, too. We both laughed and blamed it on Jack whose energy, she said, was strong and chomping at the bit. We had a great meeting, Jack coming through strong with loving messages and even responding to questions. When I was done and turned off my phone, I saw Jack's computer immediately showed it was connected, but mine was not. I had finally had it with all these computer glitches and wanted to know what was up. It was important to me to get my computer working again, so I ran it over to the Geek Squad to drop it off and have it checked out. When I came back three days later, they said they could find nothing wrong. They even played music on it constantly for three days, twenty-four-seven, straight though three shifts each day in the repair shop, and it was never interrupted once, nor did it have any shaking of the screen. I am glad, however, that I recorded that crazy, jiggly screen while it was happening.

****

Another opportunity to catch some crazy activity came soon thereafter. We had eight canister lights installed all around our lanai five years before and never had a problem. One Monday night, four of the lights on one side of the lanai weren't on, but the four on the other side were as bright as normal. Since they are all in a series on one electric line, this made no sense unless there was a short at some midway spot or four lightbulbs all blew out at once for some other reason. I called the electrician who couldn't come till that Thursday. On that Tuesday night, the lights reversed. The four that weren't working were now working, and the ones that were working now weren't! It was getting intriguing to say the least. And it obviously was not a matter of blown light bulbs. The electrician wasn't coming for another couple of days so there wasn't much I could do about it.

On that next night, Wednesday, I looked outside just after dark. This time, all eight lights were flashing, and very unevenly. It looked wild so I quickly grabbed my camera and recorded the phenomenon as well so I could show it to the electrician the next day. I was thinking that the lights might not do that again when he came. I was getting smart at proving I wasn't crazy. The next day the electrician said he found nothing wrong, and they were all fine. Of course, they were all fully lit! I showed him the video of the one side out, then the other side out, and then the video of the flashing night. He ended up replacing the transformer just in case. I'm just glad that I documented it every day. I asked Jack to please let the lights stay on. So far, he has.

****

Over time, I began to add a new dimension to my interpretation of Jack's signs. I had a funny feeling that there was more intended than just the message, "I'm here." The first time I suspected more meaning was on a morning I was having my cup of coffee while watching the news. My home alarm system suddenly generated a loud warning from the control panel. It gave three high-pitched screeches, and then the alarm voice followed, "System not ready." As I was sitting in another room and a bit distanced from the central box, I knew it wasn't me that caused anything. I jumped up to read what else it was saying on the screen itself. I tried a few options, but none worked, and it kept going off. I called the alarm company, and the woman that answered said that my front window had been tampered with. I assured her the window was closed, locked, and the connecting parts were engaged, but it kept going off. She told me how to shut the system down and promised someone would be sent out for a repair call. Just to make sure I captured the alarm going off, I recorded it talking to me.

The next day the service technician came and agreed the window was closed and apparently fine. He started troubleshooting and took everything apart. He said there was a tiny tamper button that had popped up inside one of the little boxes that makes the connection, but he didn't know why it would do that. He reset it to make it stay down permanently and told me it should be okay. He also said he'd never seen that happen before. Now the night before the alarm system had done all its warnings, I had gone to bed without setting the alarm. I simply forgot. Jack had always been a stickler about remembering to do that and, as long as he could, he double-checked on me whenever he would come to bed after me. I had a notion that he wanted to let me know he was watching by bringing my attention to it... and that he did. I was recognizing that his signs might not all be just "hellos" from beyond, but sometimes meaningful and perfectly-timed efforts on his part. It was the accompanying context that validated the message. That's what comforts me and convinces me it's him. Ever since, I have not forgotten to set the alarm.

****

One last picture that surprised me was of my daughter and me standing by the Christmas tree at her home the week after Jack passed. The person that took the picture took several in a row, called a burst. In the very middle of that series is one picture in which there's a white round area covering my daughter's neck to her heart like an orb. It isn't in the pictures before or after... just that one, and we never moved during the shoot. I've heard a white area or swath of energy can represent Spirit, and I believe he was with us that day. Christmas was his favorite day of the year.

****

I have learned to take pictures and videos of everything that seem weird or oddly coincidental. And just to be honest with you, I still don't automatically jump to the conclusion that every squeak or blip in the house is him, and I typically start out thinking there's an explanation for everything that does happen. After all, lights can blow out, and alarms do short out, but it's the meaning, timing, or combination of the events that make me take notice.

As I've said before, several of these efforts were somewhat upsetting at first until I started recognizing his handiwork. Gradually, I have learned to see the half-full glass and have gratitude for his reaching out to let me know he is not gone.

"A human being is a part of the whole, called by us "Universe", a part limited in time and space. He experiences himself, his thoughts and feelings as something separate from the rest - a kind of optical delusion of his consciousness.

The striving to free oneself from this delusion is the one issue of true religion.

Not to nourish it but to try to overcome it is the way to reach an attainable measure of peace of mind."

-Albert Einstein

Chapter 3 –
Not So Funny at First!

After so many signs and messages this past year, and all the tears of sadness and gratitude they have given me, I am finally so happy I don't react as fast anymore. What I've discovered is that most of those happenings last just long enough to get my attention, and then go back to normal. In fact, most have never happened again. If I had been open enough to recognize this sooner and had the patience to wait them out, I could have saved myself a lot of phone calls to service companies. As for how these signs from the other side happen, I have no idea, and I'm not sure how we could know that with our limited brains. And if I had just transitioned into energy in the hereafter without my body, I don't know how or what I would do to get someone's attention if I really tried. But I do know I am impressed with those times when the context points at Jack. I feel such delight when the signs are his kind of irony or humor, even without my being able to fathom how he does them. I now picture him cracking up laughing as he surprises me from the other side... finding creative ways that he knows will let me know he's there. I have come to believe he's truly enjoying himself, and I know they all come from a more Divine Love.

Once I experienced enough unexplainable happenings, I became so curious about energy in the afterlife. I started reading a lot of books by credible authors and was especially interested in those with medical or scientific backgrounds who wrote about our continuing consciousness. I looked for cited clinical support, rigorous scientific research, and validated, evidential documentation. What I have found is a consensus of beliefs about the change of energy from the lower frequency of a dense physical body to the higher, lighter frequency after the physical body ends. I learned how quantum physics has proven that all things consist of subatomic particles of electromagnetic energy and are interconnected. Ancient cultures and modern science alike have defined the concept of communication between physical and afterlife energy in terms of faith or scientific means, acknowledging it is what gives the "spark" to life. From my own experience, and with all the supportive readings I've done, I've learned how our consciousness continues through our physical experience and on into our afterlife, complete with the essence of our personality and memories.

Another commonality of these writings is the understanding of a literally indescribable place of beauty, love, creative intelligence, and of Oneness. It seems understandable that those who have "died" and come back to report what they witnessed often say they wanted to stay there. I even asked Jack, if the magnificence of the hereafter is so immense, why wouldn't he just "take off" and float away? In an instant my mind had his "pop-in" answer: "Love." What a simple thought, and it so satisfied me now knowing I can't know all that I don't know.

For those people who experienced an observed clinical death and came back, their reason typically was because they weren't done. They shared the idea that when we are in the physical state, we are here for a reason, so we need to embrace this experience in the highest of energies that we can. Our purpose is to try to live in the present and grow more kind, loving, and compassionate while we're here. Jack was all that... and with a sense of humor.

Yet there was his serious side which I felt when I was going through our accounts. He was a big tipper, a big believer in charity, and known to be extremely generous. One day I was looking at his recent business credit card statement which was canceled after he passed. It had most of his automatic monthly charges listed, and now those accounts had to be closed. I started calling one organization or business after the other to let them know he had passed away and that these accounts would no longer be needed. As I was dialing one of them, I immediately felt a "push" impact on my chest taking my breath away, and it stole my total attention. It wasn't a pain, just a strong, centralized pressure, and I wondered what was happening to me physically. I realized that I had been dialing the phone number for the Wounded Warrior charity, which he felt so committed to. It occurred to me that he would passionately want me to continue giving to that worthy cause. So, instead of canceling it, I called and put it on my credit card in my name. That's when the pressure lifted.

A few days later, I was in the bedroom going through his belongings in his chest of drawers. As I opened his jewelry box and saw his special pins, watches, awards, and other meaningful jewelry, I got that sudden chest pressure again... just as powerful and just as attention-getting. I snapped the lid down instantly, and the pressure went away just as fast.

Because I recognized that punch of energy to my chest from the last time I dealt with something very important to him, I felt it was Jack trying to get my attention again. I just found it hard to believe that his jewelry was that important to him anymore. Then I remembered how often we talked about what we had that we wanted to make as a special gift after we passed. We never put them in our wills; we just told our daughters what our wishes were. The only two things that mattered to him were giving his grandfather's ruby ring to go to our older grandson and his gold engraved retirement watch to our other grandson, and I hadn't done that yet. It made sense he'd try to remind me, but I needed to have a talk with him about how he was using his energy! He had always been a passionate guy, but he really needed to pull back on whatever surge he was doing to get my attention. I told him, "If you're aiming your energy at my chest to communicate with me, it was too much, and it worried me. Are you able to cut back, or refine that forcefulness, or find another way to reach me? Just please don't stop trying!" I gradually found that the new sensation of *feeling* something from him was exciting once I understood it was him trying to communicate. And talking to my husband out loud to the air around me seemed strange, but I assumed he was there listening, or at least aware of my thoughts.

Sure enough, that night I was reading about a husband who crossed over. His wife missed him so deeply and fell into a dark hole of grief. Eventually she began to recognize his presence through his signs and messages, and she began accepting the fact that he might not be gone. At that point in the book, my right ear started ringing so loudly that it made me stop reading. It made me laugh right out loud. I also remembered what we learned about the spiritual significance of the right side of the body to be interpreted as the male energy, and the left represented female energy. It was him! I was delighted, and relieved, that he had found a better way to say, "Hey! I'm right here, so near that I can affect your ears with my frequency."

Ever since then, when the ringing in my ears suddenly gets very loud, I notice whatever I'm doing. I feel he's sending me a message to pay attention. It's so comforting to know he's that close to me... within my space. Sometimes it's a little deafening, but, after all, he always was a passionate and powerful guy.

****

Another time Jack found a humorous way to let me know he was around when I was a bit rattled driving the car. As I've already explained, I am not a confident driver, and he used to drive me everywhere there were superhighways or long trips. This time, because I had to keep an appointment traveling a considerable distance on a busy expressway, I was wishing he was there with me. My emotions were already high, and my knuckles were white as I clutched the steering wheel to keep up with the high speed of the traffic that I wasn't used to. So, when I saw a dashboard light come on, one that I had never seen before, I panicked thinking it might be serious. I found a place on the shoulder of the road and pulled over. I immediately took out the manual from the glove compartment, thinking the worst, and started looking for that icon that was lit. When I found it, the manual described a warning light that was supposed to work in conjunction with another light that wasn't set to operate. I never remember turning either of those buttons on to notify me. I started the car back up, a little shaky, but that light was no longer lit. I had to admit that my panic was totally unwarranted. Tears rolled down my cheeks as I was missing him, and I told him how much I really wished he was with me. Before finishing my mental request, I read on the display the name of the song that had just played on the radio, *I'll Be Watching You.* I didn't know the song or the lyrics, but the title alone was perfect. It felt like he and his sense of humor were right there.

****

Jack always had such a love-hate relationship with Amazon's Alexa. He would ask Google and Alexa a question at the same time and found Google to answer instantly while Alexa would often say, "Hmmm I don't have an answer for that." He'd mutter, "Dumbass," and Alexa would say, "That's not very nice." Sometimes Alexa would follow his question with one of its own, asking if he wanted a particular service, and he'd never answer. One time he called out a question to Alexa to see when Father's Day was going to be that year. The light lit up in attention and then just went off. Alexa just didn't answer him. He also always wished he could be "the voice of Alexa" and make up wild answers to questions his friends or family would ask.

After he passed, every now and then, Alexa would make that soft *boing* sound out of nowhere without being set up. There was nothing to follow as a notification either, so it made no sense. I was never sure if it was Jack, but it was weird and didn't happen to other people I asked. There was one night when I was really feeling lonely and weepy and missed his company so much. It was 9:00 pm, the time we had set Alexa to give us our daily reminder so we wouldn't forget to take our evening medications. On this particular night, when the reminder came, I gave the typical command, "Alexa, stop." There was a pause and, as usual, the light went out. However, about five minutes later, the reminder sound suddenly went off again for no reason. It was weird and had never happened before. I repeated my stop command and Alexa, once again, got quiet. But later, as I was getting into my television show, Alexa sounded the reminder again. I had to chuckle to myself feeling like Alexa had a mind of its own, so I unplugged it and left it unplugged for a couple of hours until I went to bed. As you can probably guess, when I plugged it in around 11:00 pm, Alexa sounded that notification again... like a "gotcha!" This time when I pulled the plug, I decided to leave it powerless for the whole night. I smiled as I went to sleep feeling like Jack was playing a game with me to keep me company, and I was thoroughly enjoying it! In the morning, with an almost happy anticipation of enjoying more of our little cat-and-mouse game, I plugged it in. Alexa was now normal. It had felt like she had been possessed... by a funny guy!

****

Lights that would not turn off or would turn off unexpectedly seem to be getting more common, and I was getting used to not reacting immediately. I knew things would probably go back to normal if I was patient. I also found an immense appreciation to be able to recognize his presence and interaction. For example, Jack had given me a remote mailbox gadget with a light that goes on inside the house when the mailbox flap has been opened outside. One day, I saw the little red light was on, so I went outside to the mailbox to get the mail. When I came in, I went to turn off the light to reset it, but it wouldn't go off. As much as I tried turning it off, it stayed lit. Recognizing it as a possible new sign a little sooner than I had considered in the past, I just unplugged it for that day and then plugged it back in the next morning. The light was out, and it never did that again. Another time, the overhead motion sensor garage light went on when I went in to get in my car. It was set to stay on for ten full minutes but went out in just a few seconds, leaving me in the dark. I got into the car, sat there for a few minutes, and the light suddenly came back on with no movement at all. That made me giggle. I was learning to wait him out and was grateful for our moment together.

****

Jack seemed to have an affinity or an ability to affect certain lights now that were at times meaningful to me. Late one evening shortly after he passed, I was dealing with a long Social Security application process after a full day of other official business. I was just so tired, and without him there to pull the reins in on me as he always did, I was just pushing through. That was when the light directly overhead went out. I figured that whether it was a sign from him or not, I was calling it quits for the day and went to bed. The next morning, when I turned that light back on, it was fine. Other times, when I needed a nudge, or a reminder, or a warning, a light would start to flicker like crazy. I would think I needed to replace the bulbs, but the bulbs never burned out. Even the printer LCD screen, which is dark when "sleeping," would suddenly go on for no reason. I'd check the manual to see if it might have had a reason for lighting up like a motion sensor, but I saw that it wasn't supposed to happen. Then I'd remember I had asked him to tell me he was still around earlier in the day.

About a year after he passed, I was faced with experiencing the Christmas season without him. All of you who have had to spend the first big holiday alone after your loved ones have passed surely know this to be a really hard time emotionally. It was time to pull out all the decorations and hope they'd work, and that I'd be physically able to do it. This year, the hardest part was the lifetime of memories that suddenly flooded into my mind knowing we would have them no longer. We both used to have Christmas week off until after the New Year, and we filled it with so many lifelong traditions that we fully enjoyed. I especially remembered our wonderful Christmas Eve traditions with our girls as they grew up and multiplied into families. And, after they went to bed or went home, we'd turn down the lights and enjoy our traditional romantic slow dance by the lit Christmas tree. We'd turn on Johnny Mathis and rock back and forth to *O Holy Night* and feel so closely connected.

I always work to pull myself out of glass-half-empty thinking, so I reminded myself that I needed to celebrate the holidays for those around me... finding the joy in making new memories and feeling his love around me whenever I was missing him. "Fake it till you make it" was one of my mottos, and this year it became my focus for my neighbors and for my family. Taking a big breath, I began to pull all the Christmas decoration containers out of storage and brought them into the house. I started untangling the outdoor lights and getting out the ladder, the outdoor extension cords, and the timers. Once the lights were all spread out on the floor inside, I plugged them in, and they were all lit. I was so grateful and proceeded to take them all outside to start decorating. The first string was to go around the front door. Once it was all arranged and connected, I turned on the timer, but the lights on one half of the string were not working. It was very discouraging, especially after testing them to make sure they were fine--it made no sense. I asked Jack for help as I was taking them all down. "Please, honey, can you help me? Can you use your unexplainable energy to make them all work?" I was easily frustrated as I rearranged the lights so the ones that were working were wrapped most of the way around the door, with the non-working lights neatly balled up and tucked behind a plant pot nearby. Thrilled I had found an easy solution, I plugged it back in. This time, all the lights lit, including the now-ball of lights that were previously dark behind the pot. I stuck a Santa in the pot over them, which lit up like a happy accent to the job. I thanked Jack for his help!

As I went inside, I sat down and turned on my reading lamp. It started flickering wildly for about a full five minutes and then just stopped and was fine. While it was flickering though, I did not get right up to go get a new bulb as I would have in the past. I also didn't just wait it out, either. I decided to sit there appreciating our moment... feeling totally absorbed in his love as we shared this space and time together.

****

One of the most surprising things that happened to me that has remained unexplained was the strange activity of our pool vacuum. In the summer, I swim every day because it helps me become more mindful as I do my laps. The vac is connected by a long hose that I navigate around as I swim back and forth, avoiding it easily since it goes so predictably slow. One day, without me knowing it, it suddenly sped up from the usual crawl and raced from behind me, moving through my legs and passed forward in front of me. It momentarily startled me as my first thoughts went to what snake or critter was in the pool with me. From that moment on, it seemed to follow me around the pool at this new high speed. Whatever way I turned; it would turn. If I would stop and stand still, it would head straight for me. I began to giggle while trying to swim, and that isn't easy. I still can't explain how the speed on that machine picked up so dramatically and then went back to slow and steady. I even watched the recording of that incident on the outdoor camera to see if it was my imagination. It was so funny to watch as it seemed to have a mind of its own. I could just imagine Jack enjoying himself thoroughly, and I enjoyed the playfulness, too.

****

I must admit, I'm always impressed by every one of those amazing synchronicities as true efforts on his part, even if he surprises me. I've realized that some of them, like the energy chest pressures, the car engine lights, and the house alarm sounds were strong attention-grabbers, none of which ended up causing me a problem or a cost. All through our lives together, he loved to tease me, surprise me, and share his naughty sense of humor to make us laugh. I don't think I would believe these messages were from him if it weren't for that unique personality coming through. For example, one evening I heard a huge bang in our guest room. I didn't see anything in the room when I went in at first, but when I opened the closet door, the life-size dummy I had made for a class project and stored on the shelf had fallen off. It had been lying there flat for years, and I couldn't imagine what kind of effort would have to be made to propel it off right now, and from a perfectly stable shelf. The feathers were one thing, but a five-and-a-half-foot dummy? I did know that it represented a lot of laughs we had with it over the years. I figured he was reminding me of those happy times.

"When something vibrates, the electrons of the entire universe resonate with it. Everything is connected. The greatest tragedy of human experience is the illusion of separateness."

-Albert Einstein

Chapter 4 –
Frequent Frequencies

*M*usic can be so emotional, tying together the memories of experiences and people to the associated feelings. Music can cause us to fall into an instant response anywhere and anytime, from euphoria to despair once that call-back connection is made. And when one is suffering a major loss, it's sometimes best to turn off the car radio if you want to arrive at your destination with dry eyes. I have recently learned this. But, thinking I had the power to handle it, when the songs would come on, I would find myself on a drive of Music Roulette, never knowing if the next song would remove my peace and makeup.

I can't for the life of me imagine how the energy of a loved one on the other side can possibly affect what plays on a radio, but the coincidences amaze me. I figure the people hired to choose the playlist must be more proactive and committed to that schedule rather than making a choice based on a "nudging" from an energy field around them. But can a loved one's frequency interfere with a radio frequency? Or are they sending a thought into your mind to pay attention? All I can tell you is how I've become amazed by the synchronicities of the songs that seem to play in answer to my very specific needs. I sometimes feel like Jack speaks through the songs on the radio. At one point at the end of this year, I started looking through my journal at the names of the meaningful, attention-getting, or timely songs that played while I was driving, as well as the emotional questions that I would ask Jack just before they'd come on. The context was what made it so amazing. When I would miss him so terribly and asked for a sign, his favorite song for me would play, *You Look Wonderful Tonight*, or mine for him, *The Power of Love*. They both played so often it seemed disproportionate to all other songs, but, at that time, I felt it was crazy to believe he had anything to do with it. One time I was missing his love and feeling not at all special to anyone, and the radio played *I Will Always Love You*, reminding me he was still loving me. And after that, the radio played *You're Still the One*.

Another morning I had been meditating and imagined his energy was around me. I felt flushed with its warmth, and surprised it stayed with me. Later, as I headed out to do errands in the car, I asked him for a sign to let me know if he was still near me. I got into the car asking him, "How do I talk to you? Where are you?" As I started the car, the radio started playing *Right Here Waiting for You*.

One afternoon I told him that I hoped all the pain he had in life was gone now without that body. He was an I'm-going-to-live-forever guy. A type 1 diabetic of fifty years, undergoing chemo for chronic lymphocytic leukemia for the second time, and congestive heart failure, just to name his major chronic conditions. His peripheral neuropathy was excruciating, but the amazing thing about Jack is that he never complained. He was one of the most positive people I've ever known. In fact, he had no feeling in his feet and stepped on a nail once, driving it through his shoe and into his foot, and he didn't know it until he tried to take his shoe off. He said, "I'll bet that hurt." Even his doctors all said, "How are you alive? I can't explain you!" He willed his life to continue! After I spoke to his Spirit in the car that day asking how he felt now, the radio started playing *No Scars in Heaven*. I thanked him for his message. I had been crying and needed to clear my eyes before I went out to lunch with my friends. I asked him to pick, if he could, something happier to make me smile. The radio then played *Girls Just Wanna Have Fun*. I laughed right out loud. I mentally thought, "You're like no one I've ever known... even now!" And the song that followed that thought was *Simply the Best*, something he always joked about himself with a big ole smile.

****

Recently, I looked through the journals I'd been writing since he passed away. I knew writing every day would serve me to get my feelings out. Even better, I would be able to look back over time and see the progress I was making. I did and I was. I noticed how often I gradually started picking up on the signs, as well as interacting with him as the timely or relevant songs played in the car. I had accepted that they appeared to be responses to what I had just asked or what I was feeling. After a while, I kept a pen and paper in the car to write down the songs at red lights so I wouldn't forget them. I could see these synchronicities or "answers" were so much more commonly accepted in my journals now.

Here are some examples. The answer to my question about how he was doing was *Almost Paradise* and then *I Can See Clearly Now*. One day I had thoughts wishing he could've lived longer, or I could have kept him alive longer, and the three songs that followed, one after the other, were *If I Could Turn Back Time*, *The Circle of Life*, and then *Celebrate Me Home*. One time when I was feeling alone and missing him as my protector who always made me feel safe, I heard *I'll Be There for You*, followed by *Just the Two of Us*, *I Keep on Loving You*, and *Everything I Do, I Do It for You*. I had been really hurting that day and on a long car ride, but I felt better after he just showered me with his musical messages of love.

One of my most powerful musical experiences happened one morning as I started out driving to the grocery store. The car radio started playing a song with lyrics Jack had said to me in tender moments... Ed Sheeran's *Perfect*. Those words hit me like a gut punch and made me quickly press the media button to turn off the song so I wouldn't sob another tsunami. The problem was, no matter how many times I pressed everything to change songs on the radio or go to the CD player, the music continued to the end of the song, and so did my tears as I pulled up to my store and parked. When the song finished, all controls worked, every button and every knob. I got the message—it was for me to hear from him. I sat in the parking lot with tissues in hand, feeling him near me and absorbing his love.

That evening I had just started watching a Hallmark Christmas movie when the television went black. The power light was on, but there was no sound or picture. I changed the station to a detective show, and the television was working fine. When I went back to the Hallmark Channel, it was still black. I knew it wasn't my television, so I waited as I have learned to do, and eventually the show came back on... but well into the movie. What I discovered later was that the first part of the movie that was blacked out was about a woman losing her husband and being grief-stricken during the holidays.

When my television started playing, it was totally past the sad part and into the rest of the happy end of the movie. This time, I felt he saved me.

****

Many of my friends and doctors shared a common piece of advice for my first year of being a widow. "Don't make any major decisions for the first year after losing your husband. They would be emotionally driven, and you might think differently later." So, after that "required" first year had passed, I gradually did begin to turn the corner and put more joy back in my life. I was having more positive thoughts about getting out, seeing people, and finding a purpose or passion. I figured the work I did with clients in the fields of life coaching, school counseling, and clinical hypnotherapy should have given me enough tools to move forward and adapt to my new normal. One day I mentally asked Jack for his support and strength to help me be happier and avoid dropping into such deep sadness. I knew my health could be affected positively if I just tried and at least smiled more. The songs that played immediately after that request were *Baby When I See You Smile*, and *If It Makes You Happy*. I laughed and told him, "Your song choices are so perfect. I am not surprised with what a strong communicator you were while here physically and even now in your afterlife." The next two songs were perfect: *If You Don't Know Me by Now* followed by *That's the Way I Like It.* The next day I got into the car to go to the cardiologist, and I asked him to please be with me. I said I'd try to raise my frequency with happiness to try to meet his higher frequency halfway. *I'll Be There* came on before I could finish asking.

I don't know how it works or how I could possibly deny this is him. I see now what I used to call "coincidences" and recognize them as signs as they happen over and over again. I know I just have to stay open to what seems way too coincidental and then trust it's him. Even as I was thinking about how I've come a long way distilling coincidences from signs, Cher's song *Believe* came on.

****

I had always heard of radio frequencies, microwave frequencies, and electromagnetic frequencies as examples of unseen energy of different wavelengths. Electromagnetic frequencies (EMFs) are described as radiation from electric and electronic equipment. Experts measure this radiation to see if appliances and electronic equipment like office computers are safe to be around. Interestingly enough, because everything considered to be made of sub-atomic particles of energy, a Spirit's presence would also be detected by this meter—

though don't ask me how. I'm sure you can imagine how thrilled I was with the EMF detector I received as a fun gift from my daughter one Christmas. It was my newest toy. I read that it could detect the electromagnetic frequency of Spirit, giving me a happy gift of hunting Jack's nearness or his Spirit's presence. I loved it. At first, I did baseline readings around my home. I wanted to see if any of my appliances or technical equipment were giving off that dangerous radiation which would display with a forty or higher. I found no indications of unsafe radiation anywhere I went. Next, I started walking from room to room with this gadget to see if Spirit energy was around and/or would be readable. The detector showed readings in the blue safe zone of zero to thirty-nine. I knew that if the radiation was forty or higher, then the screen would be red and flashing with an alarm.

I checked around me while sitting in my chair and it read zero. I went into our bedroom, and it showed a zero. I'm not sure why I pointed the detector at our bed (what was I thinking?) but it was also a zero. Alongside our bed is a nightstand with a picture in a ceramic frame of the two of us kissing at our wedding. As I pointed the detector at that picture, the screen shot up to a red, flashing 188 and the alarm was going off, indicating Spirit energy was there. My heart started pounding. It was so exciting to determine a concrete reading! I wanted to shout, "I finally have proof!" I kept pointing the gadget all around, over, behind, and under the picture, and every reading was a blue screen showing zero. I even went outside to see if there was a reading of EMFs on the other side of the wall next to that photograph. I came back inside grinning from ear to ear. Pointing it back directly at the picture, it was once again setting off the alarm with another high reading, but nowhere else. Frequency from the other side was clearly there, I had to admit. I did this over and over just to see if it was still there, and though the readings were all different, there was always an alarm and a red, flashing light. I loved thinking he was right there with me, right then. That alarm was music to my ears. Speaking of frequencies, one day when a friend was over and the conversation was about how she was missing her spouse, too, I showed her my handy little electromagnetic frequency reader. I had planned to show her how it would go from a blue zero reading near me to a red, flashing alarm in the bedroom as I would go near our picture. Instead, right as I turned it on to show her the zero reading where we were both sitting, a bright red flashing light, a readout of 144, and an alarm all went on right there between us. We both wondered which husband's Spirit set it off... or maybe it was both. After she left, the detector went back to zero.

****

Jack had always been my go-to person on the computer. He knew more and always taught me new things. Now that he is no longer able to help me undo whatever I've done, my problems can seem overwhelming at times. I'm also finding that some strange things occur then go away like they never happened—it's so similar to those other unexplainable events, like with the lights or thermostat. Since he crossed over, I have come to believe some of the unusual computer happenings might not be all my fault, like that pulsating red blob, the crazy jiggling screen, and the problem with no Wi-Fi connection that BestBuy proved did not exist. I figured that maybe I could give him some credit now. For example, one time I turned on my computer, went into my email, and saw a reply from a life insurance company. I clicked on it and my computer generated a woman's robotic-sounding voice reading the email out loud to me. I laughed but had the feeling of "big brother" watching me. I had never heard a voice read an email to me before, and I certainly didn't click on anything out of the ordinary. It seemed crazy. I have since learned it is called a text-to-voice feature that, to this day, I wouldn't know how to make happen if I tried. I shut down the computer, and started it up again, and no one was reading text to me out loud anymore. Other than getting into my email, I hadn't turned anything on, and I hadn't turned anything off. Maybe he was still teaching me in a new way.

YOU DON'T KNOW *JACK!*

****

I now look for combinations of "forces" coming together to create context by giving more meaning to the messages. After taking care of Jack at home for many months at the end of his physical life, I had damaged my left wrist and right thumb. After all, he was six-foot-three and over 200 pounds. A few months after he passed, I scheduled the corrective surgeries. The first would be on the wrist, and later the thumb. Neither operation was going to need anesthesia because the local shots would numb the areas sufficiently. As I was awaiting the first surgery, and they were attaching all the lines to my heart, I mentally asked Jack, "Please be my guardian angel through surgery today. And I'd love a sign to relax me if you could. I hope I'm not asking for too much, but I'm very scared. Thanks, honey."

As soon as I did that, the nurse noticed the heart monitoring machine stopped working for a few minutes, and then it suddenly started up again. She said, "That was strange. I've never seen it do that before!" My heart felt fine, and I was reassured. And right before the surgeon came into the room to start the second surgery a month later, I asked for Jack's reassurance and another sign. At once the giant, bright surgical light overhead went out for a few seconds, and then right back on. I was so grateful for him helping me feel peace and protected. His sign alarmed everyone prepping in that room... except me.

****

Then there was what would have been our fifty-third wedding anniversary, and I was trying to remember that he was with me energetically so I wouldn't fall into a pity-party about him being totally gone. I was finding that it was getting a little easier to enjoy memories of our anniversaries without deep sadness. I especially felt so happy looking at the pictures of our big fiftieth, which was such a wonderful day that our daughters had "gifted" us. I had hoped for a sign from him all day on our anniversary but wasn't aware of any. I also have learned that strongly wishing or focused willing for a loved one to send a communication doesn't necessarily work. Whenever my busy mind tries to figure out how to make something happen, it preoccupies my brain with those thoughts, so it's hard to relax and just be open and receptive. Besides, since it was apparent that Jack's personality crossed over with him, there never was any way I could make him do anything until he was good and ready.

That night I wasn't sad, but maybe a tad disappointed. I was working on the bills and went into his office to get a postage stamp. I noticed both of my ears ringing like crazy. I also noticed the LCD light on the landline phone across the room suddenly came on, but the phone hadn't rung. The light went back off and then came right back on, and then eventually went off. In between, I quickly checked the other remote phones around the house that connect to the same system, and they were all dark—just his office phone was lit. I checked for any calls. No calls, and no caller ID indication of any call. I was so curious about how that could happen. I turned around to leave the room and saw the light come on the printer control screen across the room, but it should have been black and asleep. Soon it turned off and went dark. And that was when the house alarm sounded for a window in his office that said, "Office window open." That window was closed, locked, and not touched under the shade that I had pulled down earlier for the night. All put together, my ringing ears, the phone, the printer, and the window alarm joined together with me right there in his office on our anniversary night. I loved that synchronicity made it so clear. I whispered to him, "Happy anniversary, honey. Your signs were the best present ever! I love you, too."

****

Sometimes, there will be only one, impossible-to-explain event... no context, no other coincidence. It just can't be explained, except that it *just is*. Late one night, as I was watching television in my living room, the center of Jack's dark brown leather recliner across from me was suddenly lit up with a beam of bright, warm, golden light, shining like a spotlight on the seat and the back of the chair as if the noon sun was pouring in from a nearby window. The problem was... it was dark outside, all the windows and doors had their shades drawn, and the room only had two low lights on. I can't explain how that light could be so clear and strong and last only for a few seconds. I sat there staring at his recliner for a while longer imagining how that could happen, and grateful for his visit. It was a first... this time he came through as the Light from the other side.

"The intellect has little to do on the road to discovery. There comes a leap in consciousness, call it intuition or what you will, the solution comes to you and you don't know why."

-Albert Einstein

Chapter 5 –
The "Hi-Jack-ed" Reading

I have a friend, Yvonne. She was my fifth-grade student who ended up coming back as a teacher in my school district at the same time I continued to work there as the school counselor. We were not only peers, but soon close friends. Over the next few decades, our friendship grew to defy a relationship definition, and we saw it as just two loving souls connected. My husband also adored her, as her second father and friend, working with her to edit his books. They both enjoyed teasing each other whenever they could. She and I talked almost every day, leapfrogging to take turns listening and helping each other from our hearts. Jack would come into the room while we'd be on the phone and throw in his two cents to kid with her and make us both laugh.

So, when I got a call from her one day after Jack passed telling me he had "pushed through" during a reading she had with a medium on a Zoom call, it was not a surprise, but thoroughly exciting. "Bobbi, you won't believe what happened today! Are you sitting down? Jack came through! I'm not sure about some of the specific pieces of evidence that this medium shared, but her description of his comments was so Jack! She even knew that the name of the 'father energy' was Jack! And she held up the notes of what she was receiving as we got started to prove it."

My only answer was, "Oh, my God! Are you kidding?" I knew it could be possible because Jack was a very strong communicator, a passionate guy, and certainly saw this reading with our close friend to be his opportunity to reach me through her. My knees felt weak, and I sat down, so excited to hear from him. How it all came about was very interesting and very validating. Yvonne's friend knew this medium, Gail, who offered to do practice readings to help herself develop her skills. Once Yvonne agreed, the friend set Yvonne and Gail up to meet and do a reading on Zoom shortly thereafter, and it ended up being a bit of a surprise for Yvonne. As they were joining their Zoom meeting, Gail scribbled a few notes of her incoming impressions and then showed them to Yvonne during the reading. She later held it up to the screen for Yvonne to capture a picture of the notes. It further validated that what came to Gail was Jack pushing through. Here's what was on that paper:

"male... mustached, big strong... 'Jacked,' funny person... witty, good sense of humor... head pain... love of my life... hair salon... dark hair... man... fifty- to sixty-year-old... dad... big guy... light-headed... Jack... 'love of his life'... he's helping from the other side... penny dates... dream visits... phone crazy... don't feel bad about getting hair done."

The following quoted text comes from Yvonne's actual voice-to-text transcript of much of the reading itself. Gail began by explaining how her readings work, and then how they help others.

"To know that their loved ones are not off some faraway place in the clouds. That it's... a vibration right around us, and it's just a matter of... like... turning into it... so just like we have our physical senses, we have our spiritual senses... and that's how we connect with our loved ones... you know, the signs they send us and the little knowings that we have, the little inklings that come through... so, when I'm connecting... very symbolic for me... so they'll use my frame of reference to try to get me to say something that will make sense to you that you'll understand... so, it's really like a three-way flow of energy. Just be open 'cause you never know who's going to come through... just remember they can be talking about themselves and Spirit, or they can be talking about you or other people physically here around you, too, so keep an open mind. So, as I go... if you could connect with... yes, no, I don't know... it helps to get that energy flowing."

The reading continued with Yvonne's mother and then her father coming through, but then the "dad" energy changed. Much of what was then coming through was not resonating with Yvonne about *her* father, but she began to realize the identifying information was more like my husband's. Gail described the man coming through as a "big, very strong man, and lightheaded." Yvonne told Gail her friend's husband just passed and his name was Jack, at which point Gail remembered that the name had come to her earlier, and she had written "Jack." She had also written "jacked" on her notes, thinking the man was "jacked" as in built. They then both realized he was popping in on the reading, so Gail invited him in. This information and what followed proved to be so much more aligned with Jack. Not only was Jack a big guy, always lifting weights and trying to stay strong, but he also was very lightheaded in the end. Yvonne knew this to be true. She checked in with me briefly almost every day, and in the last six months of his life I would describe where we were when Jack passed out, and how I handled it. He had great difficulty with something called orthostatic hypotension. Basically, he would pass out when sitting up or, especially, when trying to stand up. If he even tried to transfer from the bed to a chair or a wheelchair and was up for more than seven seconds, he would pass out until I raised his legs to get blood back into his head. He did this several times a day, making it clear that Gail was connected to his energy now for sure. She also said:

"I don't know if he ever had a mustache, but you know, he was almost like that big version of, like, the Marlboro

Man, you know what I mean?" After the reading, Gail described how she "saw" him... how the vision of him came through, if he's now in Spirit without that body. She explained that our loved ones send images that relate to the medium's life experience, as she had said before, and then her job is to work at interpreting those visions (clairvoyance). She pictured the Marlboro Man as the one that had the mustache, but it didn't have to match every detail. I told her he was big and tall, but no mustache. She explained that image was from her frame of reference and was delivered as an overall impression. As it turned out, he actually did have two big "Indiana Jones-type" hats that he always wore when he went golfing every week, and they did look like cowboy hats. In fact, his favorite pictures were of him, with his big hat, standing so tall by our young grandsons when he took them golfing. And a year later, Gail asked me to check any Halloween costumes with a mustache. Sure enough, there was a wig and mustache given to him as a joke by our daughter right before he was to start chemotherapy!

She went on:

"I also wrote 'hair salon,' something about hair salon... maybe she should not feel bad about going to get her hair done."

And just so you know a little more background... that very morning I had been standing in the grocery store with a box of hair color in my hand, wondering if I should try a little color that wouldn't be permanent in case it didn't look good when I was done. At least it would wash out. Having turned naturally grayer over the pandemic and unable to leave the house to go to the salon, I was now wrestling with it. I was wondering if I really did want to start coloring my hair again. Jack would always tell me not to worry about what others thought about turning gray. "I love who you are even if your hair was purple. Do what makes you happy. But, if you do want to color it, do it right. Go to a professional salon." So, this validation from Gail absolutely blew me away. I had told no one that I had just started considering it. Only he knew, which meant he had been "with me" at the store that morning. It meant he "saw" me or knew my thoughts as I stood right there reading the directions on that hair color box. I was over the moon loving all this undeniable evidence!

Gail continued with her reading with what she was getting from Jack for me:

"I'm gonna be around you... I'm still gonna be helping... you and the kids are gonna be fine. I don't know if there was one [kid] in particular that I was especially worried about, but he wants to do everything he can from his side to help with that. If that makes sense... if you pass those messages on for her. And he's the one... I mean, he is turning lights on, making her... you know... like doing all sorts of things for her, and I just got chills, so I know it's him. Yes, yes... I... I really feel like he's very strong... he's gonna be helping her a lot, and... and... the more he helps her, the more she's acknowledging that the signs are from him... the more... you know, she'll get them. Okay... and he connects with—what I was going to say, a butterfly—but then he corrected me and said, 'no, dragonflies'... so, to look for dragonflies from him."

As I read this transcript, I knew immediately what he was talking about and was so relieved that he'd be watching and helping. Yes, there seemed to have been dragonflies all over the place around my yard in particular, and I was glad he owned up to being the one playing with my lights. It confirmed my beliefs, and that's when I began to see the importance of sharing with my family how their dad, or Pop Pop, was communicating with me. I wanted them to feel free to open their minds to possible signs showing his love and support for them, too. If it brought me so much peace and comfort, why would I keep it to myself? Gail continued:

"Okay, yeah, I think he's coming through because he knows you're so open and that you will be open to giving her the messages to let her know that he's around her and to validate... and dream visits, too. He's gonna try to come in dreams... if she hasn't had one already. Her phone does... she's gotten crazy things on her phone, too. Um... yes, she's been having problems with her phone and fax machine... he's going to do everything he can to help her... so, yeah... thank you, if you could pass that along to her."

Gail continued to speak to Yvonne about a variety of images she was receiving:

"He's showing me a significant gold engraved watch and a purple plant. And does a ringing in the ears mean anything? I really feel like Jack was really wanting to get through to your friend, so I hope that you'll pass that along... he was up like a force, and you know he was well known for his sense of humor and a big strong guy."

What is so interesting to me about this reading was that Yvonne and Gail did not know each other before the reading, and it was Jack who came through Yvonne's reading for me... totally unexpectedly, and with some amazing validations. There could be no question about the medium having any advanced information. Yvonne knew nothing about the watch, plant, hair coloring, office phone, and fax. Gail was so amazing at bringing through such private personal experiences that no one could know but me. For example, about a month before that reading, I moved one of the plants I received at Jack's Celebration of Life event to a new place by a window and noticed it was too big for its pot. It was a gorgeous calla lily blooming in all its glory. I had decided to transplant it to keep it alive, so I went out to find just the right decorator pot, got the right potting soil, and proceeded to really get into it up to my elbows. It had been an especially sad time, so I fought off the tears as I shopped and worked. In the end, I was happy just to have gone out with a purpose without crying, and accomplished something that made me happy. When Gail mentioned working with a purple plant, I knew only Jack could have witnessed me do that, since no one else knew that the plant I had just repotted was purple.

Gail made a reference to a gold watch with an engraving which was equally amazing. Jack reminded me often over the years that he wanted our younger grandson to have his engraved gold watch. I found a gold watch in his jewelry box and delivered it feeling I had carried out his wishes. Not long after, I was in a small drawer of his that held special keepsakes, and there was his solid-gold engraved dress watch. I had totally forgotten he had that watch, and I realized I had given the wrong watch to that grandson. I immediately told the grandson what I did, told him to keep the old watch, and to put Pop Pop's special watch in a safe place. There is no way Gail could have known about the significance of that watch unless Jack "told" her.

Gail also mentioned the crazy phone in Jack's office-and it was crazy. I described earlier how his business phone stopped recording voicemails immediately after he passed. The message indicator would show how many messages were left, and I would hear the phone ring, but there were no audible messages. The fax machine also stopped working right after he passed. Jack gave the message to Gail to tell me not to worry about it. We had always been so protective of one another over the years, and this reading told me he still was. Worrying about people not getting a response from him and hurting his reputation was no longer important to him. He wanted me to know it was okay with him to relax and let it go. It was a wonderful validation of his continued love.

****

There have been times in my life when I have had a medium read for me. My first time was right after my dad passed. Prior to his passing, I had gone to visit him after he had done all the chemotherapy and radiation for cancer and was given a terminal diagnosis. We had one of our last conversations in which I swallowed hard, held back the tears, and said, "Dad, I've always told people how proud I am of you, and I've bragged to all my friends about what a good man you were. I'll always love you." At the end of that conversation, he just got quiet and thanked me. I realized I had never told him that before, and his thoughts about that or about dying must've been racing through his head right then. There was quite a pause, and I felt a little sad that he didn't say he was proud of me, too, but I reminded myself that this conversation was about me being able to say goodbye to him. It was to be my last opportunity to tell him whatever I needed to express. Whether he was proud of me would have to remain unknown.

About a year after his funeral, I decided to speak to a medium. I didn't have any experience with spiritual readings, but hoped she'd at least get a message from him such as, "I love you, I'm fine, and be happy." Much to my surprise, Carole, the medium, gave me so many validations that it was him and his personality by using the way he spoke to give information about my family and career. The best one was when she told me that he said, "I've been trying to reach you. I see you, but you don't acknowledge any attempts I make to let you know I'm still here. It would be easier to contact you through Ma Bell. And I want you to know I *am* proud of you and it's important that you know that." That reading was so comforting.

****

Another time, when I went to my friend's house for dinner, she introduced me to her friend who seemed to be distracted by something right away. "Hi," she said with a certain urgency and, looking preoccupied, she apologized for what she was about to ask. "Sometimes I hear from Spirit, and they persist to be heard even when I try to make them leave me alone. I'm getting a 'mother energy' from the other side wanting to come through for you. Have you lost your mom recently?" I told her that she had just passed away four months earlier, so I was all for it. This friend said this mother-energy was coming through to tell me that she loved me, and that she was so sorry she couldn't feel love when she was alive. She explained that she had too much fear in her life that got in the way, but she could feel love for me after she passed. It was alarmingly true for the relationship we had. It was also quite comforting to know that the mental illnesses experienced during a physical journey no longer exist on the other side. There was nothing left for her to fear now, it's all about love, and she found a way to let me know. Now that I understood she *couldn't* love me, but did now, this reading became a life-changing moment assuring me it had never been about who I was, what I did, or whether I was worth loving.

As soon as she was done giving me her message, the woman told me my mom wanted to prove she was right there near us, right then, and asked her to take a picture of me. My friend took a quick series of pictures of me standing up against a dark, solid wall away from windows or lights. On one of the pictures was a big swath of white light right near me, but only on one picture and without my moving or any other changes during the burst of shots. I was impressed. The woman seemed relieved that she was able to deliver her message, and I was delighted to get it. Later, as I got into my car and started the engine to leave that night, the volume on the car radio was blasting the song *I Will Always Love You*. I turned the volume back down to where I normally keep it and whispered, "Thanks for trying so hard, Mom. I love you, too."

****

Many years ago, Jack and I took his mom to get a reading to see if his late father might come through for her. Trish was our medium and we were very impressed that she studied under John Edward, the man we had watched doing readings on television for years. She was so ready when we got there, declaring Jack's grandfather, who worked for the railroad, had been keeping her awake the night before. She kept waking up with visions about how to lay train tracks and filling her with railroad information she couldn't know just to prove it was him. Trish proceeded to give all three of us messages from loved ones besides Jack's grandfather. My father came through with a private hummingbird reference, and eventually his dad, too. Trish told his mom that his dad said, "I'm here with Elizabeth." I saw his mom suddenly had no color in her face. It turned out they had lost a child many years prior and had wanted to name her Elizabeth. Jack's mom's eyes filled because she knew Jack's dad was there on the other side with Elizabeth.

****

I have so much gratitude that our loved ones try so hard to come through. I don't know how they find their openings or opportunities. I am also grateful for those people who are the mediums, the messengers, who work to develop their gifts. Mediums help people connect by teaching how that energy works. They say you can practice mentally "hearing" the messages from your loved ones through clairaudience. During the year after Jack passed, I did "hear" his voice in my mind when I was quiet. It took some time for me to allow the possibility, discern his voice from my own thoughts, and recognize the synchronicity or timing of his messages. Trusting that it *could* be him, and then realizing it *was* him was a bit of a process. I discovered that any thought that comes from outside of me and arrives when I least expect it can be from Spirit. Mediums suggest that these communications occur at times when our minds are relaxed and more open. And they seem to be non-linear, like in a whole different direction. Thoughts from Spirit are interruptive, like "pop-ins," and not produced by our minds. My personal and most common receptive times for this are when I'm waking up in the morning and whenever I am meditating. It's when I am not busy-minded and can experience that subtle discernment. What helps is how clearly those interrupting thoughts come packaged in Jack's low tone of voice, unique blunt style, language, or sense of humor. We always thought, spoke, and acted very differently, so he definitely distinguishes himself from me!

****

After Jack "hijacked" Yvonne's reading, I was so impressed with all of Gail's validated evidence that I made an appointment for a reading with her for myself. I was able to record that reading and will share that next.

"I didn't arrive at my understanding of the fundamental laws of the universe through my rational mind."

-Albert Einstein

Chapter 6 –
A Strong Communicator

Soon after Jack passed, I started thinking about having a medium reading, but was overloaded with more immediate business to attend to. I also wanted to be able to pay attention without crying, and that would have been quite a challenge those first few months. As the weeks went by, due to COVID, the two readers I would have gone to weren't available. I did eventually go to a John Edward event, but I knew in my heart Jack would not come through because so many others there needed to hear from a loved one to let them know they were there. I was feeling blessed that I had the communications that I did. However, a few months after Jack hijacked Yvonne's reading, I couldn't wait any longer. I asked Yvonne for Gail's email address and made an appointment for my own reading. I wanted relief from the aching inside... missing him so badly and yearning for any and all communications possible.

I absolutely couldn't wait for my Zoom reading. I was more than hopeful that Jack would come through, knowing him. His signs had been prolific all around the house and in the car, so I wholeheartedly believed he would continue to reach out. Gail introduced herself and shared, "I've always been intuitive and recently had a surge and an awakening, so I've really opened up to it."

She continued to describe how her readings work, the same way she did with Yvonne, with drop-in thoughts, three-way energy, and minimal validations. She then let me know Jack was trying to get started, recognizing his energy, and she had to ask him to wait. I was sorry Gail felt rushed, but secretively tickled he was already there and ready to go! Gail led us through a little prayer of grounding anyway, and then admitted that he was too excited to wait any more. She said:

"Okay, so I'll take a deep breath. I feel like he's saying, 'It's showtime!' like he's a very strong communicator... um... very outgoing, fun, lively, fun guy. I know that... and as he comes close... he's wanting to hand you a bouquet of fresh flowers. So, I feel like that was something in life he was known to do... he would bring you fresh flowers often to show his affection. He was very demonstrative with his affection for you... um... known for, like, his big hugs."

As she said that, I really choked up, but knew I had to keep it together. As a big guy with arms that would wrap all the way around me, his hugs were complete, safe, and so missed. And in our later years, Jack would always have flowers sent to me with candy and balloons for our anniversary and my birthday, and he'd make sure that it was the biggest arrangement they had. He believed you should never skimp on presents.

"Big hugs, lots of love. I feel like his family was everything to him. His girls... he's calling you his girls... family first with him... like that was just the way he was.

He also just talks about... that he doesn't want you to dwell on the moment of his passing, but he wants me to mention it. He's saying he knows there was no formal goodbye, and he's sorry about that... but couldn't have done it if there was any other way. He couldn't have left if he had to say goodbye to you. So, I feel like he's saying that you understand it."

As Gail shared that, I flashed back to our last evening together. That night, after watching television, I set up the bedside table with all the things he might need. I leaned over him in his living room hospital bed to tuck a pillow behind his back so he could stay sleeping on his side. As I did, his arms wrapped around me, and I melted into him. He spoke in a quiet voice, "My heart feels really tired tonight."

I wasn't sure what that meant but took his blood pressure and said, "Then let's just take it easy tomorrow, okay? No physical therapy or any exercises."

He said, "I love you." I kissed him and told him I loved him, too. Gail said:

"He tells me you talk to him all the time and he hears you. I feel like you say good morning to him, and you say, "good night, Jack," when you go to bed at night. And I feel like he had a nickname for you, too... like with a B, or Bob, or Bama... did he have some kind of nickname for you?"

I told Gail that my name is Bobbi, but he'd sometimes call me The Bobbi Lama.

"Okay, so what else... I just... as I feel into him... I feel a very strong work ethic with him. I feel like he knew how to work hard, and he also knew how to play hard, so as hard as he worked, he had a lot of fun, too. He always wanted to make sure there was a balance. He tried really hard as a man to make a balance between his work and his family. But he wants you to know, in his heart, his family was first and foremost for him, always, always... He's saying that expression... uh... 'happy wife, happy life.' Did he used to say that?"

I answered with a laugh, "Well, I guess we just knew it. If either one of us wasn't happy, the other one would feel it." "Yeah, he said, 'If Momma's happy, everyone's happy.' That's what he was always... it was like a joke. Just really a lighthearted, happy person... uh... you know... I don't feel like he took things too seriously. When he was a doer, he was dependable. I mean he'd get things done. And that was just the way he was... and I feel he's still like that and into everyone around him."

I let her know she was hitting the nail on the head with each perfect description. She was able to give me so much evidence that she was connected to his energy, and I loved learning how his physical time spent with me was appearing as his personality now in his new frequency.

"He was a good motivator at what he did... he wasn't one to mince words. He'd just say it as it was... but he had a good way of communicating with people that he was interacting with... like he would know how to say things to people without hurting their feelings but getting his point across. So, in that way I feel like he was a real good leader, and I feel like he was a real good mentor, too... that a lot of people looked up to him... uh... not just family, but around work... I feel like around work... that was very important to him... uh... like, mentoring people."

I jumped in, wanting to let her know how valid her impressions were. I shouldn't have talked so much, but I was so excited and wanted to explain. "And that's what he did for a living. He was a trainer, and at the end of his forty-plus years of being a technical trainer and giving classes, he won the Spirit of Independence Award posthumously for the highest contributor of a lifetime of giving to his industry. It was announced, running repeatedly on a jumbo screen at the international convention after he passed. He had become an actual legend in his field, so, he was honored beyond his wildest dreams for exactly that!" Gail continued: "Okay, so that's why he's bringing it up, and as you're saying that I'm getting all flooded with goosebumps... so, um... lots of pride there... lots of pride like my chest wants to be filled with love. Oh, okay, so that's why he's having me talk about that so much. That's an amazing accomplishment, and that's something he's very, very proud of... absolutely."

I told her how thrilled I was that he knew and felt the reward of his efforts, even if not until he was on the other side. I had been feeling so deeply sorry that he never knew of that award, and now I am overjoyed! He did get to know his value from his journey on earth having given so much to make such a difference for so many others.

"Okay, so that's such a perfect validation of what's occurring now... currently... and I love when they do that. They'll drop in things that you're doing, or he sees happening to let you know he's not gone... he's still here. They're very much around us. People sometimes think they're, you know, they're gone... a million miles away in the clouds... but they're not. Heaven is right around us.

They're just in a different frequency, like a higher vibration. So, to be able to tune into it, um... that they're right here... right here... and he wants you to know that. He's right here... like, I feel... do you feel that? Do you feel like a little touch?"

I told her, "I actually had to ask him *not* to do what he was doing, which was a pressure on my chest because it was too much. So, it's changed over to a loud vibration in my ears. When I hear it vibrating very loudly, I just know he's right here. He always was a powerful energy!" Gail said:

"Yes, yes, okay... and that's really awesome that you are open to it, and you're both acknowledging it." I shared with her, "We both trained in Reiki, learning the 'feel' of energy, and we enjoyed doing energy work. He always promised me that when he crossed over, he would reach out and give me signals and do things to let me know he's around. And he's been doing a lot of things recently, like my computer just now was acting up when our Zoom time was approaching. So, when he does these things, I'm learning they will eventually work later, but he's, you know, his energy is just interfering with the computer." Gail continued:

"I love this, because this is such a good validation for me... how he's such a strong communicator, because you're both so open to it, and I truly believe that's how it works...

so, it's awesome that you guys are both so open to it, and he's such a strong communicator. And that totally makes sense that that's how he was able to slip right into Yvonne's reading that day without me having any clue."

I joked, "He used you. I'm so sorry, but I'm so grateful!"

"I am, too, because I need confidence. This is good for me because I need to really... he's a good person to practice with. He's very clear. I love it. And he's letting me practice with you. And I guess that's the teacher in him."

I agreed. "Oh yeah, he's happy to teach anyone who needs him. And something else I wanted to ask. Yesterday I had the television/phone service repair person come to fix a cable line—that worked fine when he got here, by the way. I explained to him how my television had our personal phone number pop up on our caller ID information on our TV screen, on and off for a few days, like Jack was calling me, and then stopped. There were no phone calls or ringing, and the service guy had no answer... he could not explain it. Was that Jack's doing?" Gail replied: "That's Jack! Okay, let me get back... Um, okay, so let me feel back into him and see what else he's aware of. I feel like there's congratulations in the family coming recently... some kind of award, some kind of celebration with the family. A granddaughter? He says, 'I'll be at the wedding... I'll be at the celebrations.'"

I exclaimed quickly to validate that, "Yes, yes! One granddaughter just graduated, another one is about to, and our oldest granddaughter's getting married in October. He always promised her he'd be there, dancing at her wedding!" Gail continued:

"Let's see... uh, so I feel there were a lot of vacations, like at the beach... and the sand... and a lot of good times... uh, like, I just got a really relaxed feeling, like chilling out at the beach. And do you still go to the beach, and do you feel connected to him when you're at the beach yourself now?"

I answered, "I don't go to the beach much anymore, but we did all the time. We used to live in a beach town and took walks on Sunday afternoons on the beach and took most of our vacations to beachy places. I live right by a pond now, and I sit outside where we used to sit for the last fifteen or so years." She said:

"Okay, okay, yeah... I feel like when you're outside in nature, uh, he's bringing you by the water and that was a very good place to kinda meditate and clear your mind and connect to him.... on the bench, like next to you. You feel him alongside you? He's saying to put some of his ashes at the beach."

I told her I did feel him near me there, and I intended to do that.

"What else? I just feel like such a tremendous... I know you said when he comes close, you feel a heaviness in your chest, but I'm feeling that, too... and I have so much... he wants you to know how much gratitude he has for the life he had with you as his wife. That he's so grateful that you chose him, and he's so thankful that he chose you... that you two were, and still are, and always will be like two soulmates... and you know that... uh, and he gets a little more quiet and a little more serious when he's talking about that.

In the beginning he was more kinda like, uh, joking around, but I feel like he wants to be more serious about this, and for you to know, like, soulmates are real, and you really are soul mates. And he's really so grateful and so full of gratitude for the life that you two created together. It was, like, I feel like it was a perfect life you two had... um, it was just... it feels like it was always never failing with you two. I want to say, you were the bread to his butter."

Once again there was a huge lump in my throat and tears started. "Yes, we were very close."

I was thinking back to when we first met in college on a Saturday afternoon. I felt so connected and attracted to him instantly. We went to the library to do homework for our first date that night and walked around the campus sharing stories of our lives till the early morning hours. Sunday morning Jack came to my dorm bright and early to walk me to church and spoke into my eyes, "I finally found you. Do you know how long I've been looking? When we get married, we'll have two kids, a white picket fence, and I'll have a rose sent to you every day from work. It will come at a different time each day, so you'll be surprised." We both laughed about the rose, but not about the rest. I knew we were supposed to be together, too, as if our souls had already made that deal, and he was my person for life.

"Did you used to... like, was there a joke about a 'Honey Do List'?" I laughed. "Oh, my goodness, yes. He didn't like it when I made a list of what needed his attention and then handed it to him at the start of the weekend. I learned he wanted me to just tell him as the week went along so he could plan his own precious time off. A good lesson for me.

He always let me know straight out what he did and didn't like about something, but usually added a funny twist to keep it light." Gail continued:

"Cause he's, like, rolling his eyes... yes, I feel like he was always keeping everyone around him laughing. That's... I feel like that's, now that he's on the Spirit side, he can see

115

that part of his job here was to raise everybody else's vibration around him when he was here by his energy... like he just had that energy, that uplifting energy that people were drawn to... that light that people were drawn to... um, uh, what else?

And I really feel like at the end... I feel like there was a lot of confusion around what he had to take and when he had to take it. I don't know what happened, or... but there was a lot of confusion and I feel like he's thanking you for helping him, like, balance it all out. Does that make any sense?"

I agreed. "Oh, my goodness, yes, he had so many medications, and they kept changing them and changing them. We had seven different trays, and every single day, to be done at different times, and the doctors kept trying to find the better ones. It was a nightmare for him. Plus, he couldn't see that well, or even stand up, so I just did it for him. The funny thing was, even as I would do his blood sugar and blood pressure readings before the meds and the meals, he would be making jokes to keep me smiling. I always felt we made a good team." Gail said:

"That's what I feel like what he's saying... it was very confusing, and it was hard trying to balance them, but you did a really good job trying to keep him... keep him organized and keep him calm about it, even as it got overwhelming. Yeah, totally a team... uh, so, he's thanking you for all that help and support in sorting it all out. So, that's what he wants to say about that. So, in a way, what he wants me to say is... he's not happy he left you, but, in a way, it's kind of a relief that he's not in all that confusion anymore... he wants to blow you a kiss about that."

I felt so appreciated at that moment, knowing he valued what I had done, and I completely understood the relief he described. I added, "We met when we were nineteen and twenty, so we had fifty-four years together. He had a lot of conditions in the end, and we worked together tirelessly to keep him alive. I just hope he didn't suffer or die in any pain. Can you share anything with me about that?"

"And I'm getting all goose bumpy when you say that... what I feel is he just kinda went to sleep and kinda slipped away... like what I've been told, and I know this from my [deceased] son... the Spirit leaves the physical body before the last breath... sometimes when we're there, we might think they are suffering, or there was a struggle, or some kind of pain. But what I understand is that the soul, when it's ready to leave... many times the soul will actually leave the body before the last breath. That's the way I understand it... that's what I can imagine would be the same situation for Jack, too... Was he home when it happened?"

I shared that story of his last night. "Yes. He was in a hospital bed, and I had tucked him in for the night and went to bed. I woke up in the middle of the night to a loud boom. He turned his cellphone on to look at the outdoor camera app to see if it was our house. I said, 'Do you want me to go outside and check anything?' And he said, 'No, no, go to bed... I got this.' There he was, lying in a hospital bed, incapacitated in his bed telling me he'd take care of it. He said, 'Good night, I love you.' And I said the same thing. And when I woke up just a couple hours later, he was cold... he had passed, but he hadn't moved. He was still looking comfortable in the bed. So, I just assumed that he fell asleep." Gail said:

"Yeah, that's the way I'm feeling it. Basically, what I was seeing was him just going to sleep... that... just leaving, you know, just slipping out very peaceful... and he doesn't want you to think of it any other way. There was no struggle, there was no, you know, fear... it was just very peaceful, and very calm... calming... very easy. What he has to say, and he said, 'You know this... death doesn't exist... it's just a different me... a transition, yes, a different frequency... uh... it's just like stepping through the doorway. You know, from one room to the next, and um... and um, all that confusion... and, you know, everything gets left behind.'

He's saying, 'Don't dwell on that. Dwell on the fifty-four years we were together. And don't let that one moment haunt you.' And, um... I'm going to share something my son is saying, to share this with her. He said, 'Ma, think of my life as the beach, and every grain of sand on the beach is one moment of my life... don't focus on that one grain of sand when I left my body, but on the whole beach.' And it just kinda flipped it for me and changed the perspective I had, to that one moment doesn't define him."

I liked that image. "Okay, that is excellent advice and a beautiful metaphor that I can hold on to." She continued:

"Yeah, so if you're worrying about the moment Jack left... I feel like both my son and your husband are saying to tell you that. So, Jack is proud of the strength that you have had your whole life, and I also feel like now he's on the other side... I feel like whatever you do from here on out is going to be even stronger because you're going to have him helping you from the other side... um, it's just going to go to a whole new level of your Reiki and your spiritual journey and your spiritual work."

At this moment, with this message, I felt like everything just changed for me. Instead of feeling without him and his love and strength to support me, I felt the opposite. His love was undoubtedly coming through, and now his strength would be there as well. The best part was his assurance that he felt it was the right time for me to expand and make a difference for others around me using all I knew and all he was helping me see. The seed was planted for my new purpose in life. I was so grateful that my shadow was lifted. Jack and I have found a new way to be a team, now.

"Are you aware that one of your granddaughters is very connected and feels and hears her grandfather? Do you know?"

I guessed, "I think the older one, uh... I don't know exactly how my granddaughters are connecting with him spiritually, but I know they believe in it. My oldest one sees things that she feels are him and his signs." Gail continued:

"Yes... okay, that's validating, then... yes, that's what he was saying. Maybe he'll keep encouraging her to acknowledge because he feels like he's getting through to her. So, it is him. I feel like he's going to be messing with her cellphone, too."

I laughed. "He does mess with my head... he does things on our thermostat and the navigator system sometimes... it's just constantly somewhere."

"The electronics, yes! It totally makes sense when you think about it because we're energy, and we're vibrating at such a high frequency, so I'm sure if you're in Spirit, and you don't have this dense body holding you down, then you can use your energy to manipulate the energy around you."

That made sense to me. "Right. And I knew he would do that. He promised me. He said that I know energy affects energy, so not to be surprised. I just warned him not to turn the power off in the house 'cause you're going to scare me'. So, he plays with the thermostat, but lets the air conditioning work. He just has it give error messages, and when I call the company, they say it doesn't make sense, or is not possible." Gail said:

"That's so funny. That's awesome though, that he's such a strong communicator. Hmm...let's see. When you said, like, AC... I'm seeing... I'm wondering if it's something with Atlantic City, like, did he enjoy going to casinos or having fun, like in Atlantic City?"

I jumped in, "No, he didn't gamble, but AC is for air conditioning. His whole career was in air conditioning. That's what he received that highest honor for. It was for the HVAC industry."

****

I learned so much from Gail. First, Jack is so clearly around me. There was so much that he communicated with her that only the two of us could have known, which told me that he had been watching me. It was such an amazingly true evidential reading. Secondly, I love that his personality and memory have undoubtedly crossed over with him without any competition, judgment, or negative feelings of any kind... only pure love, and that is so comforting. Thirdly, I realized what a pain I was while Gail was doing the reading. She had asked me not to say much more than yes, no, and I don't know. I got so excited about being able to help her feel the amazing validation she deserved. I did way too much over-sharing. What I learned is that she had to concentrate on getting back to her open state to feel Jack. She had to work to get rid of her personal thoughts that were generated by all the information I was giving her. My bad, and lesson learned. At the end of the reading, we just began to chat some more with me letting her know some more supportive background for what Jack communicated. He loved music and had been sending me so many messages through songs on the radio, so it didn't surprise me. Gail's last words were how grateful she was that we were both so open to signs in the afterlife, and that he was such a strong communicator. I thoroughly agreed!

"A human being experiences himself, his thoughts and feelings as something separated from the rest, a kind of optical delusion of consciousness. This delusion is a kind of prison for us, restricting us to our personal desires and to affection for a few persons nearest to us. Our task must be to free ourselves from this prison by widening our circle of compassion to embrace all living creatures and the whole of nature in its beauty."

-Albert Einstein

Chapter 7 –
Natural Wonders

I was always fascinated by books and movies about the butterfly, like Robin Williams in *Patch Adams*. That they are symbolic of transformation, and therefore signs from our "dearly departed" who have transitioned to the afterlife. But my husband said not to count on him representing himself as a fluttering butterfly. I found the concept hard to imagine, too, knowing his manly demeanor and nature, but what I've discovered is how synchronicity can play out. For however his energy, his personality, and his higher frequency can impact creatures in nature, I was witnessing several non-normal events that seem to have too many coincidences. In fact, after Jack passed, I was working late into the night. I saw a small brown moth with a teeny, little notch cut out of one wing circle around me, right near my head... around and around, almost touching my face and hair. I tried to ignore it at first until it made its fifth or sixth circle very close to my eyes. I looked up, realizing it was not being drawn to the light of the lamps in the room, but to me... my head. I had to laugh as it landed on the chair next to me at the dining room table where Jack used to sit, and it just stayed there. It didn't fly away for quite some time as I continued working. As I finished up my work and stood up, it flew off the chair. When I headed into another room, it went with me, alongside me, and then disappeared from my sight. The next morning when I got up, I walked into the bathroom and saw that moth, with the little notch in one wing, lifeless on the bathroom floor.

I've never had a moth in my house before, but it's not impossible. So that alone would not make me think it's a sign. It's also more likely a moth will fly towards a light than to fly towards me away from the light, but again, not necessarily a sign. I've also never had a moth circle my face, up close, over and over and over again, which was where I got suspicious. And I've definitely never had a moth sit by me and then fly beside me from one room to the next. All these coincidences put together, along with Jack's sense of humor and his promise to make it interesting, made me feel him affecting the energy around me. All those questionable happenings put together created a synchronicity that was too hard to deny. And synchronicity suggests you pay attention to animal or insect meanings. I looked up "moth symbolism" to discover it represents transformation, renewal, and believing in your intuition.

Another time, I was sitting with a friend by a window when we both saw a moth light up, reflecting the sun coming in from a nearby window, and start going around my head. As it continued, I told her about the one shortly after Jack had passed. I put out my hand in front of her and, just to be funny, asked it to land on me... and it did! I was so surprised, and the shock on her face was incredible. She couldn't wait to go tell her husband.

The third moth "visit" happened a few months later when I went out to the garage to do some laundry. I opened the washing machine door, and a moth flew out... which makes no sense at all. The door seals tightly, and my last load was a hot wash with detergent and bleach. Once again, as it fluttered around me for a while, I smiled and put my hand out. Sure enough, it landed, stayed for a few seconds, and then fluttered around me some more. I must admit, those landings never cease to amaze me. I googled the brown moth some more and discovered it is good luck, especially if they land on you. Paying attention was now paying off, and I recognized that I was replacing more of my grief with seeking out signs and, with them, a positive personal transformation. This new way of looking at the continuum of life and afterlife strengthened my intuitive insight. It filled me with a new awareness of the limitations of what I thought I knew. I was so much more open to learning how communication works from the other side.

* * * * * * * * * *

Then there was the little bumble bee that paid me a meaningful visit a few weeks after the moth. Here's where the synchronicity begins to build with the backstory of Jack's horrendous experience with bees as a kid. Back in those days, he and his friends always got together in an empty lot to play ball. One afternoon, one of his friends made a homerun hit and sent the ball flying into a tree where it got stuck. Jack ran over to the tree to retrieve the ball, not knowing that there was a huge bees' nest in that tree, and that the queen must've been threatened or killed. In either event, they were angry! In defense of their queen, that swarm from the hive engulfed him, stinging him repeatedly and creating a cloud of bees around his head as he ran blindly away from the tree. A neighbor saw the event, called to him, and used the nearby fire hydrant hose to force the swarm off him. He collapsed and was taken to the hospital where he went into a coma. They put him on an IV and pulled stingers out of his eyes, face, hair, and body for several days. So, to say he had "a thing" about bees is an understatement. Whenever there would be one buzzing in his area, he quickly moved away swatting vigorously. And if there was ever one in our house, I was the one to get rid of it. We transplanted all flowers and flowering shrubs on our properties every time we moved to a new house. One time, we had to transplant several amazing rosebushes to the edge of our backyard just to keep the bees they attracted away from our doors and walkways. It was no surprise that this horrible memory could affect such a big, strong man for the rest of his life... but not his afterlife, as I will share.

One really cold morning in January, a month after he passed, I went out to my mailbox to put some thank-you cards out for the mail carrier. As I went to lift the red flag, a bee flew by my hand and over in front of my face. I shooed it away thinking how surprising it was to see a bee in a temperature near freezing. I was even more surprised that it kept flying around me as I was walking towards our side yard. It stayed around me while I did some cleaning and eventually followed me to my front door. I did a real dance trying to avoid it coming into the house with me, but it slipped in anyway. As soon as I saw it was flying around the foyer inside, I opened the door again, and started moving to go outside. I saw it follow me out, and then I zipped back inside, slammed the door, and gave that little guy the slip. I was so impressed with how that bee stuck with me so long, right near me, Jack's most dreaded insect in life, and in such unlikely weather. Timing and meaningfulness created the context to make me notice the synchronicity.

The second time a bee made its presence known was to a longtime friend of mine. She and her husband used to visit with Jack and me, and they both enjoyed Jack's sense of humor and stories. She remembered him sharing the one about that swarm event and thought of him when she was out by her pool and a bee was flying around her for an unusually long time. It made no sense because there were no plants around her for it to be attracted to. Being a medium herself, she got quiet, closed her eyes, and she received a strong sense that it was Jack's energy trying to get her attention using that point of reference. She asked him what he wanted. When she called me, she said that she could mentally hear him answer, "Call Bobbi, she's fragile." When she called that day, I had just been crying so hard and feeling so alone. After we spoke and had a few laughs, I felt so fortunate that Jack was sharp enough to communicate that way... a little bee message to a friend.

****

There were my hawk events, too. One flew to land on a fence that ran alongside my backyard. It was unusual that it faced my open back door where I was standing. It perched with its back to the pond whereas hawks usually sit there with their backs to me as they scan the water for food. It simply sat there facing me. I moved outside very slowly towards the hawk, expecting it would take off as soon as I got too close. It just sat there facing me, even as I walked away from the door and toward it. I continued to walk out into the yard getting nearer to the side of the hawk, and it just sat there facing me, moving its head to face my new position. As I got closer than I ever was able to in the past, it finally took off. Now I'm sure that could happen—not typically, but it could. The reason why I felt it was more than just a coincidence was because my medium reading that happened earlier that day included a comment about watching for hawks as a symbol of Jack still being my protector from the other side.

It happened again while I was out for my morning walk the very next morning. A hawk flew over me and landed on a fence of the house I was passing. It totally watched me as I approached from the hawk's one side, just staring intently with its head swiveling at the neck to keep looking at me directly as I walked by. As I moved down the street, it took off from that fence I had passed and flew to the next fence I was then passing a few houses away. It repeated the same stare down, even when I was just a few feet away.

And the third hawk sighting happened the very next evening. It landed on a chair in my backyard and stared at me while I sat on a nearby chair. It was so close to me, barely eight feet away, and it didn't appear to be afraid at all. In fact, I was so impressed by its confident stare. It was a good thing I was told to look for hawks as signs from Jack letting me know he was watching out for me as he said he would.

****

Another bird event happened that was out of the ordinary. This time it was a common bird that populates the island in the pond near me... the ibis. Jack and I always loved to sit outside on the lanai to wait for a large group of them as they would migrate from and to the island every morning and evening. They would all fly together in large, beautiful, synchronized formation, perfectly choreographed, creating sky-filled visions. During the middle of the day, only a single bird might fly to or from the island, but not in big groups. It certainly was one of our favorite pastimes together, so it wasn't a surprise that he might use one of these birds to send me a message.

There was one afternoon I felt so weepy missing him. I had been holding it together for several days, but I just needed to cry. Now I had recently read that if I could lighten my energy with happiness, then his higher frequency would be closer to mine, making it easier to connect.

However, this morning I just couldn't stop crying. As I sat facing the window to my backyard and looking over the pond just yearning for him, I spoke to him, "I am so sorry that I can't seem to stop the outpouring. Can you please help me?" I wanted him to help me stop crying. And that's when it happened. A bird flew right into the screen of our lanai cage with a loud *thwap*! It was so startling. I had never seen anything like that or heard of that happening before. I ran right outside to see if the bird was okay. It was an ibis, one of our favorite birds. I watched it get up slowly in the grass, shake it off a few times, walk a little, and then it took off. I couldn't believe that bird was okay. More surprising was that Jack found a way to make me stop crying by shocking me out of it. He definitely raised my frequency!

****

Red cardinals are another common symbol believed to be sent by our loved ones who are trying to connect with us from the other side. When I looked up their symbolism, they represent strength or courage, and they are considered a sign that a loved one who's passed is nearby. Jack had always teased me that the males of many species, including him, are prettier than the females and he'd continue to site examples every time we'd see an "animal couple" like a pair of red cardinals. The male was certainly a beautiful red and was prettier to him than the girl cardinal, who was mostly brown. We also used to talk about how amazing it was that so many animals would mate for life and would grieve the loss of their partner when they'd pass. We watched a show one time about that, and they showed a male duck of a "duck couple" who had its wing injured and was housed at a wildlife rehab for several months. When it was healed and it could fly, it was released to the same wooded area where it was found. As it flew into the air from the cage, its mate instantly soared right out of the nearby woods to join it. It was beautiful, and Jack said he always saw us as connected forever like those ducks. With that as the backstory, I was not surprised to see a cardinal pair, one red male and one mostly brown female, swoop across a big window one morning as I opened the drapes. What surprised me was how close they flew together, and how close they came to the window—within inches. What furthered my surprise was that they flew across the whole window, turned together in sync immediately, and then flew back across the entire window again... two swoops that truly grabbed my attention!

****

About ten months after Jack passed, I went to my oldest granddaughter's wedding. I remembered Jack promised all of us when she was born that he'd be there to dance at her wedding. I knew the doctors had made him feel like his life was limited due to all his conditions and that he wouldn't make it to old age. His promise to me and to her was to stay alive and beat those odds. He did beat the odds, but didn't make it to the wedding. He had transitioned from his physical body just months before, having held out many years longer than was ever expected by his doctors. I also remembered that Gail's reading included a reference about his planning to be there in Spirit from the other side, so I was comforted by that. However, I wondered how he'd let us know and hoped there'd be no bird crashing or hawk staring. The afternoon before the wedding, we were all sitting outside taking turns posing for the photographers who were staging different wedding party groups and capturing some candid ones. At one point, my daughter saw a ladybug on my shirt and let me know. I had read that the ladybug is seen as a positive sign of new beginnings and good luck. The woman sitting next to me brushed it away before I could stop her. As the ladybug flew off, it immediately landed on my granddaughter's wedding dress. She was absolutely delighted! It stayed there for the next few hours, through the photograph session, through the walk down the aisle, the wedding ceremony, and back up the aisle to the reception. As she danced, my heart was full. There are many pictures that captured the tiny red dot against the pure white gown. I have mine labeled, "Pop Pop kept his promise!"

****

After Gail said that Jack told me to watch out for dragonflies in her reading, I did notice them in abundance in my yard. However, one day something so interesting took place and I call it "the dragonfly tree." After getting home from the wedding, I was sitting outside and looked up at a dragonfly that did its swoopy air dance around me and then landed on the very tip of a pine tree branch nearby. That's when I noticed that the huge tree had one dragonfly on the tip of every single branch... the tippy tip! The tree was loaded with what seemed to be hundreds of dragonflies. It looked like a giant Christmas tree with a tiny bow tied on the very end of each branch. It was magnificent.

****

The more I hear what others believe are convincing signs or messages from their loved ones, the more I discover the reasoning that makes them feel that way. When they are unexplainable, unlikely, or occur as coincidences, it makes sense. A friend told me her father had been a florist and specialized in roses and passed away one fall leaving his wife of sixty years. Late that winter, the rosebush at his home had a single red rose bloom through layers of snow in all its glory for her mom on their anniversary. As I've said, I initially used to challenge sign-like occurrences with skepticism until I began to differentiate simple everyday happenings from the meaningful, unexplainable, or coincidentally timed ones. Now, once I do, I embrace the experiences and give Spirit credit for trying so hard. Jack's promises to send signs to me from when he was living added to that ability to discern his signs, such as his messing with electrical and electronic devices. He sure gave me so many undeniable ones, especially when I add in his personality and our lifelong history together. The chance that it is him using his energy to get my attention becomes so strong.

****

I do have to admit, I was not that open to messages from the other significant people in my life after they crossed the way I was with Jack's Spirit. I also had never discussed what those people intended to do to get my attention from the other side before they transitioned like I had with Jack. Plus, after fifty-four years together, he came to mind constantly with everything I did. In addition, for his last months, he was the focus of my attention almost every minute of each day, so we were so very attached. With that much love, connection, and history, it's no wonder we've been blessed to stay together. For that I am beyond grateful and why I chose to write this book.

On the first Father's Day weekend after Jack passed, I stayed overnight at my daughter's house on the Gulf of Mexico. The panoramic view was breathtaking through the great glass wall across the whole back of the house. That Sunday morning, she and I were having a cup of coffee facing the water and were into a deep conversation about Jack's signs, the afterlife, her success as an independent business owner, and how I was doing. I was reassuring her how important it was for me to stay strong, healthy, and purposeful now that I was alone. Our attention was suddenly diverted to the sight of a great blue heron landing on top of a piling at the corner of her dock not far from that window. Now, for the significance of this bird, the "great blue heron" was what his grandfather was nicknamed back when he worked on the railroad in the early 1900s. He was a tall and stately man, Jack's namesake, and Jack revered him. He even bought a giant great blue heron statue to overlook our backyard pool in his honor, which we endearingly referred to as "his grandfather" thereafter. For every holiday, when I would decorate around the house and around the lanai, I made sure I decorated "his grandfather" tastefully.

This great blue heron kept our attention because of how long it ended up staying there. It was so stately and beautiful, and I know it was at least forty-five minutes before I was drawn outside with my camera and slowly walked up to it on that dock. It was so calm and didn't get spooked, so I kept taking picture after picture as I crept up close to get that perfect shot. When I was satisfied, it still hadn't moved. It just stood on that piling so comfortably. I eventually went inside the house but stood at the window watching it until it finally flew away. It must have stayed there over an hour, which was longer than I've ever seen one stay on a perch. I looked up the symbolism of the great blue heron and found that it brings messages of self-determination and self-reliance with the ability to progress and evolve... clearly a message for us both. When it flew away, my daughter smiled and said, "Happy Father's Day, Dad!"

"I think 99 times and find nothing. I stop thinking, swim in silence, and the truth comes to me."

-Albert Einstein

Chapter 8 –
My Spiritual Pen Pal

Gail had once suggested to me that I do free writing to connect with my late husband to see if he would "get into my head" with his responses. Free writing is a method of allowing whatever comes into your mind as it comes in without stopping or worrying about punctuation or spelling... just writing. She said she did that quite often and would receive answers from her son who had passed. I had read about doing that from other sources, too, but couldn't imagine it working for me. It just seemed hard to believe that my mind would let go enough, or that I would be able to tell the difference. On my first attempt to write a question to Jack, I hoped I would simply start writing his answer by willing it to happen. I said a short prayer, wrote a question, and it went badly. I could tell it was my own answer alternating with what I thought he *would* say to me. I felt like I was generating everything. Then I remembered what I was told when I had spoken with others who had that special discernment between their thoughts and Spirit's thoughts. It was important to relax my busy brain before my free writing. The second time I tried it, I meditated quietly, focusing on my breath until I slowed down my busy monkey mind, but that, too, didn't create anything that I thought was from him. I also remembered how I needed to be open without any neediness or urgency. I invited his answer as a request without pressure and welcomed any results. With that in mind, preparation for my third time gave me hope. I felt like I relaxed, stayed positive but not needy, and opened up into a higher frequency.

I started with my blank notebook and pen, sitting outside on the patio overlooking the pond where we used to have our morning coffee or our sunset glass of wine. I sat in his chair, meditated for a while with a focus on my slowed breathing, and invited him in mentally, trying to feel his energy around me. I felt my love for him so strongly. I expressed my sincere gratitude for him having been such a strong communicator, and then I felt his love around me. I set my intention to receive from him whatever he would send for my highest good, and then stayed in that positive energy and waited. This time, I wrote that first question that came to my mind...

The question I had asked myself that morning after I went into his closet. "How do I clean out your stuff?"

At first, when I started writing, I knew it was me, or at least me writing what I could imagine Jack would say to me. However, after a while, it began to be not only more his tone, but words that I don't typically use, and thoughts I wasn't expecting. Once that began to happen, I just allowed myself to receive thoughts as they just dropped into my mind, a free flow, and I kept writing as fast as I could. They weren't linear, thought after related thought, the way I would think, because there was no order. And I wasn't "hearing" as we normally expect when we use our ears. His answers were in the form of full instant thoughts... pop-ins, complete knowings that were arriving into my mind from an external source. I wrote in my own version of speedy shorthand so I wouldn't miss anything. Some phrases were funny, most were direct in tone just like Jack spoke, and I sensed they were all sincere and loving. His attitude powered his answer, but without his ego mind. There was no commanding or directing or demanding, which made sense. After all, I had to assume a loving Spirit would allow for my free will and not alter my personal lesson-learning journey. I do believe that Spirit can help or support us when we ask for it with our intention already determined. For this writing, I was deliberately detached from the answer and the outcome, which made it easier to concentrate on speed. I just wrote in shorthand what was arriving in my mind enriched by his personality, passion, and common sense. It honestly felt like a visit... a familiar comfort.

January 16, 2023

My question:

"How do I clean out your stuff?"

His answer:

"You can start by deciding what you need... what you can use. Then, give items you don't want to those who do.

Then, to Good Will.

Then toss.

I don't have a body – no need for clothes or jewelry.

Turn anything into cash if you have the energy. You shouldn't need the money; you have a house. You can enjoy the space.

Exercise, please.

I'd hate to see you in a state of pain or disability.

Let me know when you want to go, but in the meantime, find happiness and know that I am here... near.

Yvonne's right ... I'll make you look, but I am not the signs. Go with your instinct... it's a good one now. It wasn't before. Your innocence and need to believe was naive. I will help you discern and be strong.

Continue loving with your whole heart. That's it. That's what 'the All' is... Love. For you, only a limited word, but just wait for when you join me. You won't believe it... or, actually you will. You'll remember.

I love you in a way you can't possibly know. And I enjoy watching you—especially when you discover it's me... like in the church. I filled you with me... did you feel it? No need to sway and sing there... just feel me, feel it, feel the Love.

Know the eternal omnipotence of the one creative intelligence.

Be patient with the physical limitations... but keep writing to help others. Give comfort. That's the beauty of you.

I'm not gone. I see you sitting there on my chair, on the patio. Enjoy the view... all the physical majesty... and our sunset.

There's so much more to come. Trust me."

Then, just like that, it ended. The thoughts stopped arriving. I was so focused on getting everything written that when it stopped, my own mind felt like it was still off duty. He was obviously done, and I had my answer. I came back to myself, to my own thoughts, and felt a swelling of joy and gratitude. There was no doubt in my mind that he had sent me what I needed. The tone, the style, and the phrases were his. When I want to throw something away, I use those exact words. I just say that I'll throw it away. Whereas Jack always said, "Toss it." And the Sunday before the free writing, I had gone to a new church with my daughter. It was a huge production, with musical singers and instrumentalists performing and speakers that heightened everyone's attention to their faith. At one point, my chest felt like it suddenly filled up, and I was experiencing such a warm wave of a powerful Love. I couldn't explain it, but I just had a "knowing" it was Jack, and I was beaming. Adding the church reference to the other validations like his mentioning the patio, the sunset, and my writings, his answer just blew me away.

I also never used the phrase "trust me," but he did quite often. In fact, it was one of our little inside jokes. He punctuated many statements with that phrase because he enjoyed getting a rise out of me. He played the role of someone whose confidence was ridiculously strong, and he knew he was challenging me to follow up on his predictions. He'd use that phrase when predicting football games, elections, or people's behavior. He always had a little smile when he'd say it. I think he also enjoyed being wrong when he was, just to see me happy when I'd win a round. We played that little game for all our years together, and I believe he used it to validate that this answer was from him.

YOU DON'T KNOW *JACK!*

****

After that free writing, I continued to read so many books sharing experiences that validated my own. Some of the authors that I enjoyed included Suzanne Giesemann, Eben Alexander, MD, Mark Anthony, George Anderson, Gary Schwartz, PhD, Mark Pitstick, DC, Chris Lippincott, Linda Williamson, Sue Frederick, and Michael Mayo. They served as a good reminder that I'd need to clear my mind and raise my frequency to get closer to his. One of the ways I learned to shift from the low, heavy energy of grief and into a higher and lighter one was by bringing my awareness to the essence of my soul. I've learned to quiet my mind of the ego chatter and feel the Love within as part of the beautiful Oneness of our shared being... our essence. Since we are one with God, Source, Higher Spirit, the Universe, the Light, Love, or whatever word or concept we choose, we are therefore one with those lighter emotions of joy and gratitude. I believe that is the quantum energy that is all of us and connects all of us.

Focusing on that essence during a clearing meditation was what really worked for me when I reached out to Jack. This time, I wrote a letter asking, "How should I represent you in the book?" Once again, for this writing experience, I made sure I meditated quietly for about twenty minutes, clearing my mind, and focusing on my feelings of love for him to raise my energy. I then put my pen to paper "talking" to him as if he was right near me... so close that he could read along as I was writing. And once again, his answer arrived in my mind. It was so subtle, but I knew the thoughts weren't mine, and they were ones I wasn't expecting. Here was his answer:

"I think humor is key... it's what I'm remembered for... keeping life light, laughing with others was my way to connect and share at the soul level.

Write from your Bobbi Lama consciousness and name the author whoever you want. We'll know... the Universe will know... and the message will be felt even if not understood by the limited physical brain.

Find a clear and catchy subtitle if you want to grab the interested. Money is not important.

Sharing your belief with your passion is your purpose. I am secondary. Send my love." I was thinking he would have answered by just telling me not to worry about it. Instead, he was all about having it come from my heart and then letting it go where it's needed. In fact, his whole answer surprised and delighted me... especially "sending his love."

****

The next time I wrote to him, my question was, "What if the people who read this book don't believe in an afterlife?"

His answer:

"Don't worry about it. Everyone believes differently and at different times and in different ways. And then even that changes. Look at my journey.

Physical minds are too limited to understand what the All is... what the creative intelligence is... eternity.

Those who need it will read it.

Don't doubt what we are experiencing... it's real.

We're all in this together. Our energies are connected for eternity. Just write... they'll decide.

They'll all know... eventually. Share the energy of Love.

Trust me."

This time there wasn't a lot of information that seemed obviously evidential, but there actually was meaning buried in some of his simplicity. His statement *Look at my journey* carried a lot of weight. When Jack grew up, he went to Roman Catholic elementary and middle schools and was an altar boy in high school. But in college, he fell out of belief in that specific doctrine and said he was an atheist, for lack of a better word. He had taken a Religions of the World course in college and had a radical change of heart with a broader and more universal understanding. I would argue this because, after many conversations about how he changed from Catholic to atheist, he admitted he just didn't know what or who had the indescribable power to create this world, this universe. After we met, he felt his soul finally found mine and we were joined together for not only our physical lives but on into eternity. He said he then had a "knowing" of his soul and an afterlife. He eventually agreed that he was actually an agnostic and admitted he believed in something so big he just couldn't explain it. The word "God" just wasn't enough.

Fast forward further into our marriage, we started doing energy work and took classes that were more spiritual than religious: Tai Chi, Reiki, Qigong. He had an acupuncture doctor he went to for relief of some serious pain. After his father passed, he asked for signs and got them. He regularly asked for guidance from his grandfather. He meditated and opened up to communicate with his late uncles Walt and Kenny. He had no doubt there was an afterlife and that our consciousness would continue forever. In fact, he believed our physical experience is only a relatively brief interruption along that forever continuum of our souls.

So, for him to suggest that I remember his journey was a reminder that he went from altar boy to atheist, to agnostic, to Reiki Master, from communicator *with* the other side to communicating *from* the other side. He found it interesting that the religious people of the world were committed to their various religious dogmas, their holy books with their ancient masters... and yet the individual beliefs could be so different within those groupings, even arguing over different interpretations over those doctrines and holy books. His belief was that his physical brain was too limited to know for sure how it all worked, but that he had a temporary physical body and would go on into the spiritual life of energy. His belief was that we can't possibly know what's on the other side for sure, and so he said, "I'll let you know when I get there."

****

I no longer need to make asking a question in my mind or on paper such a step-by-step ceremony. I have learned to communicate with Jack now and know how relatively easy it is. I just do a mind quieting and a strong sensing of our shared Love energy. For me, that's it. I have a thought question, and I get an immediate popped-in answer that often overlaps the question. That fast pop-in thought happens so instantaneously that I usually don't get to finish the mental question. My brain seems to be so much slower in processing than his incredible speed of receiving my question and responding... all in just a nanosecond. Also, short answers don't surprise me with him... that was how he always was: to the point.

I started to ask, "Did you know you were going to die that morning?"

His answer: "No. I felt my heart was tired... I let go... slipped out."

Me: "Where did you go?"

His answer: "I was right there."

Me: "Did you see me when I found you?"

His answer: "Yes... I wanted to hold you... I was right there."

I wish I knew that then. When I found him that morning of his transition, I was holding his body as if I was "holding on" and could keep him for a little while longer. I sobbed saying goodbye that day unaware he was right there in Spirit, lighter, relieved of his body, and wanting to connect with me. If I could only have understood he wasn't really gone, that we'd still have this afterlife connection, I wouldn't have been so devastated. In fact, just knowing we can communicate has made me deal with grief so differently as my "first year" has unfolded. His signs, once I trusted they were from him, gave me so much gratitude and joy. I had my life back... a far cry from the black hole of sadness I had immediately fallen into. I wish we both knew about all of this a long time ago.

"Reality is merely an illusion, albeit a very persistent one."

-Albert Einstein

Chapter 9 –
Sweet Dream Visits

*V*ery often, when I go to bed with a problem, I say a prayer asking for clarity from my angels or from whomever can lead me to an answer or solution by morning. I remember one time when I was a school counselor facing a likely contentious morning meeting about a student whose parents were angry and ready to sue the school. As that student's advocate, and someone who had formed a good relationship with the parents over the years, I found myself in the middle, both needing to support them as well as the school policy that was being challenged. Knowing the superintendent, principal, and vice principal were all braced for quite a difficult meeting, I was trying to imagine how I would speak with my own opening, calming message toward keeping the meeting productive. I went to bed asking for help. As I opened my eyes that morning, I heard the words, "We're all on the same side." It planted the seed of thought I needed. When I was called on to review the issues in front of everyone that day, I started with, "We're all here today to work together on a plan that will help your son, so we're all really on the same side. Finding relief for him will relieve us all. We just need to stay within school policy, and, believe me, there's nothing worse for a middle school kid than having to explain to his friends why he gets special treatment or is above the law." With that, everyone laughed, the dynamic changed, and the meeting went very well. I thanked my Higher Power for the words that pulled all parties together with a common cause—and with great relief for all involved. The best part about turning it over to a Higher Power is that it takes it off my mind and then I can sleep, knowing I'll love waking up to a clear answer. And the answers are almost always ones I didn't even consider the night before and definitely not from my ego mind. I'll mentally laugh, "I wish I'd thought of that!" When it's Jack that supplies an answer now, he wakes me up in the middle of the night—I guess they don't "do time" on the other side. He was always very impatient and passionate when in his physical state, anyway. When he comes through, it's strong, and I become completely awake and clear about his answer. It's in his low voice as my mind receives it. That strongly asserted energy will make me so alert with excitement, that I'll get up out of bed to go write it down. I want to make sure it will be the first thing I see when I wake up in the morning, although I don't know how I *wouldn't* think of it right away. What I've also learned is that his visits or messages in my dreams are not like typical dreams that often fade away from my memory after a while. His messages are as memorable as if they just happened... live, using my conscious mind.

One day after I started to write this book, I realized it would be a real challenge to select a title that I felt truly reflected the essence of the story, of Jack, and of my new awareness. Another issue was that I knew he knew what it was like on the other side, but I could not begin to understand (or remember) this non-body dimension. I've observed and felt Jack's communications with a broader view of what's possible. A good deal of my overall experience has also been supported by reading authors that describe their thousands of medium readings and near-death experiences in the afterlife. And, since Jack passed, I have learned about the newest scientific studies on afterlife frequencies, too. With all this input, my understanding is still evolving. I know we are energy, and that our essence—that deep, soul-level frequency—is higher and lighter than when it is with the body and "compressed" into our heavier physical form. I understand that our bodies come with ego minds that help us survive, and those egos are done protecting the body when we transition out of the physical form. As Jack said, "Death does not exist, it's just a different me... a transition, yes, a different frequency." He also sent the message: "That's what the 'All' is... Love." He refers to "feeling the Love" and knowing "the eternal omnipotence of the one creative intelligence."

I realize my brain's limitations when trying to imagine where he is, and what eternity or infinity looks like. I assumed I would not be able to know the unimaginable magnificence he was part of now because, as he said, "...just wait till you join me. You won't believe it." And added, "Be patient with the physical limitations." Doing the best he could do from Spirit, he had been at least able to demonstrate that consciousness continues after the body dies. He also made it clear that I could validate signs by their meaning, their timing, his personality, or our shared experiences. The most overriding evidence of his ego being gone was that there was no serious competition or conflict, no ill will, no negativity in any of his messages. Thinking back on even the signs I didn't like, they all came from a strong attempt to get my attention, so I knew he was still with me. All came from love, including his communication through "imported thoughts" at a subtle level. I knew I had to be okay with that until it was my time to find out. Patience was never my strongest virtue, either, but I'm working on it.

****

I went to bed one night and asked his Spirit to help me find a great title that would solve all my issues, that it would speak to the essence of our first year of communicating from different worlds, exemplify Jack's personality and humor, and address what I can and can't understand about that other side. At 5:42 in the morning, which is not the time I usually get up, I can assure you, I woke up with a start. I was fully alert, and I received the title of this book. It was delivered with his typical bold enthusiasm: "You don't know Jack!" It was not one I would have thought of myself. In fact, I recognized his tone as I mentally "heard" him saying that phrase clearly. I could just picture the little triumphant smile on his face. And more convincingly, it was familiar—one of his typical comments for when he could see I had no clue about something. I admit, the phrase as it's known is typically longer (my apologies if it offends), but it really fit. I was thrilled to have my title after scribbling so many possibilities on scraps of paper for months every time I thought of a new one. My favorite part was that I knew it came from him. *We* were producing this book, sending this message, and he was a major contributor and my support guy from the other side! It was so him, and it said it all. I believe he was saying that when we are in our physical form, we have a limited physical brain, and we can't imagine not being physical. I picture a turtle walking slowly across an eight-lane highway outside of Washington, DC. What could it possibly know about the goings-on in our government? So it is for us on this side. We can't know what he's experiencing in this spiritual energetic state, either. We don't even know what we don't know.

****

I have had so many dreams at night about Jack, but sometimes Jack enters my mind very differently. He's not part of a story. His presence seems unbelievably real in my mind's eye. In fact, those times aren't dreams. They are more like visits. For the dream state, the subconscious mind can create quite creative metaphors that can be quickly forgotten as we wake up and start using the conscious mind. On the other hand, I've noticed flashes of images that are not only extraordinarily real, but also unforgettable and seem to arrive into my mind as if they are "sent." I had one of those alarming flashes once when one of my children was in college and was in an accident at night on her way to pick something up at her grandmother's house. I had just fallen asleep, and I was woken up with such a start. I could picture an accident scene, the cream-colored car, and my daughter. It was so clear. I could see her slumped over the steering wheel and see where the car had been smashed. I woke Jack up and shared it with him. He reminded me that I worry about that kind of thing, so it was probably just a bad dream. I certainly wasn't going to call my daughter in college at 11:05 at night to find out. I went back to sleep convincing myself that she was probably in her dorm and safe. I didn't know she had gone out. Very early the next morning, she called me from the hospital telling me of that accident the night before around 11:00 or so. It happened exactly as I pictured it. And when I read the accident report, it stated it happened at 11:05. I still remember that "flashed image" thirty years later as clear as if it just happened.

After that experience, I realized there was something going on beyond my understanding. It reminded me of how I always knew when my aunt Helen was going to call me or was thinking of me—an ESP connection that she had, too. I began to read more about frequencies beyond our physical senses, acting like radio waves that we can't see but we hear the music, like microwaves, invisible but cooking our food, or like X-rays taking a "picture." So, about six months after Jack passed, his face appeared while I was dreaming. It was his face when I met him... when he was twenty years old. It took up my entire mental visual field, and his look of love was penetrating. I have no photograph of that particular image, or know why he decided to "visit" me at that age. I was not surprised that it wasn't part of my dream. It was as real and lifelike as I remembered him in his body, and I can still see that image in my memory today. It just popped into my mind's eye, interrupting whatever I was dreaming about, stayed for a bit, and disappeared. I remember thinking that first time how grateful I was for his visit. As I was lying there with my eyes closed, I spoke to him in a whisper, "Thank you for doing whatever you had to do to make that appearance happen for me. It made me comforted that you're not gone. Thank you. I love you," and I went back to sleep.

When I woke up the next morning and was getting out of bed, I had such a big smile on my face because I could still see that face as it suddenly appeared in my mind. I still can.

I found it interesting that one of my daughters called that next day to let me know she had a visit from her dad in her dreams the night before. She said he just appeared, so real and so clear, but not talking. He appeared like he was right there... an image that woke her up and stayed in her memory, too. I told her about my visit from him and we figured his energy disperses, obviously allowing him to be in more than one place at a time, and probably "sent" as a thought. I also wondered if he probably tried to get through to both of us at other times, too, but couldn't because we weren't receptive till we slowed down. Typically, both of us are very busy-minded and focused on our to-do lists every hour of the day. He probably had to wait until we both quieted down like when we'd go to sleep.

YOU DON'T KNOW *JACK!*

****

Jack and I had some neighbors that we'd get together with every Wednesday night. They liked to smoke cigars, have drinks, share crazy stories, and bust on each other to laugh into the evening. After Jack broke his leg, had surgery, and ended up in a rehab that was also a nursing home, those get-togethers came to an end. Visitors at the hospital and nursing home were not allowed due to COVID-19. I was permitted in so I could take care of his special diabetic diet and congestive heart failure food restrictions, as they told me he was only there for his post-surgical physical therapy, not the management of his other conditions. I spent every day going back and forth with his measured amounts of protein, carbohydrates, fat, sodium, potassium, and fluids for his lunch and then dinner. I did the extended visits twice a day for two months until I was able to get him home. Even then, COVID was still a scare, and most people didn't want to come visit so as not to bring it to him. It turned out that Jack never had much of a chance to say goodbye to these neighbors. However, the day after Jack passed, one of those cigar-night couples told me they woke up in the middle of the night to a special motion sensor nightlight that had just mysteriously lit up. There was no motion, no pets, and they were sound asleep. There was no reason for the light to go on. It lit up night after night, waking them up repeatedly until they finally put it in another room. Both of them were positive it had to have been Jack's well-known rascally sense of humor coming to say goodbye. I asked them if they felt spooked by it at all, and they both assured me they loved hearing from him... except for the part where he was waking them up. They figured Jack was having the last laugh!

****

One time, I fell asleep after dinner while working in my recliner with my computer on my lap. I had a long day and I was exhausted. I had just started a legal transaction with an old account I needed to put into my name. It had taken quite a while to get to that point, but I had to wait for my computer to load a lengthy document. As I was quietly sitting there and waiting, I dozed off. The website's double-verified "signed-in time" was timing out and it would have been very frustrating if I had to retrace the verification steps I had already taken to get that far. Sound asleep, I suddenly heard a loud *"Bob!"* mentally shouted in my head in Jack's voice, and it woke me up with a start. He used to call out "Bob" to grab my attention quickly, so his tone and abruptness were clearly in my memory as him. It was just in time to reactivate the transaction on the computer before I would have had to do the whole sign-in and download process all over again. It was not a dream, but a perfectly timed wake-up call.

****

Another "save" was one morning when I overslept my alarm for an 8:00 am local doctor's appointment. I had bought a new electric clock the day before and set it that night for 7:00 in the morning when I went to bed... or so I thought. I also then turned off the volume on my cellphone like I always do when I go to sleep so all the email and text message *dings* would not wake me all night. This left me totally reliant on the new little clock. That next morning at 7:35, my cellphone made a notification *ding* despite the sound being turned off. There were no new text or email messages to explain that *ding*. Thank goodness it did because the new alarm clock never went off, and it was after 7:30. I just barely had enough time to rush to make it to my doctor's appointment. It wasn't until that night when I heard the alarm go off at 7:00 pm that I realized I hadn't changed the time of day setting from pm to am. Since that phone *ding* should never have happened, I must give credit to Jack for saving me again.

****

His third save came as a warning thought that woke me up from my sleep. It was a strong "drop-in" vision of smoke from a fire, and it interrupted a dream I was having about cleaning my pool filter which had nothing to do with it. It was in the form of a flashed image of my wall-mounted dust buster in my garage giving off smoke. What impressed me was how real it looked, and that it totally stuck with me, so I couldn't go back to sleep. When I checked to see if there was any smoke there, it was clear and no smoke detectors were going off, so I went back to bed.

About a week later, I had my handyman scheduled to come over to do some work around the house. I was writing down the needed repairs the night before and decided to just go check the dust buster again to see if it was working. It was dead, so I thought it meant the battery could no longer hold a charge. When my handyman arrived that morning, I told him the story of the dust buster dream and suggested he just remove it from the wall altogether since it wasn't working anyway. When he removed it, he found the wall was very hot right where the wires were that connected it to the wall. They had melted, and when he removed the mounting bracket, he exposed one of the wood studs that was charred black. That was such a scare, and my knees were weak at the thought of it turning into a fire. I was so grateful to Jack for flashing that image into my mind while I slept.

****

The thing about dreams is that you can't decide what you want to dream. You may have an unresolved issue that will play out in your subconscious mind and create a composite of characters acting in a way that resembles your issue, like one that replays your recent frustration, your embarrassment, or your worry. It also may not be linear or make sense. You could feel powerless in real life and find yourself in a dream on a road trip in the back seat of a car going too fast, which represents that powerlessness. The place may be wrong if you analyze it, but the metaphor can take on feelings of your unresolved problem when you wake up. And dreaming, especially when you don't wake up from them to realize you've had one, does not always leave you with a memory the way the conscious mind in a real-life scenario does. For some, the memory of their dreams can dissipate like steam unless they bring them into their conscious minds. That's why it's often suggested that we write them down as soon as we wake up if we want to remember them.

On the other hand, the "drop-in visits," as I call them, are so sharp, so clear, so real... and so unforgettable. They may be just one word, one flashed image, or one sensed "hug," as I experienced early one morning while I was sleeping. I had the flash memory of one of Jack's hugs. It was our last one, the one I've previously described as I leaned over him in his hospital bed on our last night together. The memory of this hug came to me in the form of a discernible light pressure of his energy on my back. I was laying on my side so adding pressure on my back got my attention. It was noticeable, and it was exactly where his hands used to press to hold me to him. When it felt like his arms released me, I wasn't sad. I was truly grateful because I woke up feeling loved. That was such a sweet visit.

****

Another early morning wake-up visit had me challenged. We always had a joke between us about forgetting the singer of the song *Banana Boat*. For some reason or other, I could never remember his name. Jack eventually could and loved to tease me with it. All he had to do was say *Banana Boat*, and I would smile and draw a blank. He'd laugh, wait... and nothing would come to me.

Then he would triumphantly announce the singer's name as if he'd won a contest. This particular morning, I woke up with that song playing in my head wondering why on

Earth it would be so clear. As I was lying there somewhere between a dream state and awake, I kept hearing that song in my head and, as usual, I couldn't think of the singer's name, and was feeling sad that he wasn't there for our usual joke. I then suddenly could hear Jack's voice just pop in my mind saying, "Harry Belafonte." It totally woke me up and I quickly realized I'd just had a mini visit because of how clear and real it was. I also had a good laugh... and I'm sure he did, too.

****

It makes perfectly good sense to me that I have visits from my loved ones much more easily as I'm falling asleep or waking up. That drowsy alpha brainwave state is a time when my mind is very relaxed and therefore more open to receive incoming "dropped-in" thoughts. It's a little like when you're driving on a long trip on a boring turnpike stretch and your mind wanders, almost hypnotized by the road and the repetitive motion. You're not as interactive, highly alert, and engaged as you would be in busy city stop-and-go traffic. It's why all the mediums that I have talked to or read recommend that we meditate to quiet our minds to receive messages from Spirit... to try to get into a monotonous lull to get ready. I know that as I wake up slowly, I pick up on messages or images. But after I've fully revved up my "busy mind" beta waves, my thoughts really pick up speed, and the to-do lists start playing. At that point, it makes it too hard to receive subtle thoughts as they mix in with my busy brain activity. I try to take advantage of that relaxed and receptive space at either end of a night's sleep to invite communication from the other side. I can tell now when thoughts or images have been sent to me or dropped in and are not generated by my mind. I have so much gratitude for this gift of discernment, and for the lasting memory of each visit.

"Our separation from each other is an optical illusion."

-Albert Einstein

Chapter 10 –
My September Reading

*T*his medium reading, I was a smidge better behaved, but definitely not perfect, I admit. There were a few enthusiastic explanatory validations, but I tried to restrain myself. I reminded myself the night before Gail and I were to Zoom to try to stick to mostly yes, no, or I don't know... or at least keep it very minimal and only to validate and only after she gave me the message first.

Feeding any information would make us both wonder what came from Jack and what came from me. Also, the night before, my expectations were so heightened, and I spoke to him out loud, "Oh, honey, I'm so excited to hear from you tomorrow. Please use that passionate energy of yours to make it easy on Gail. I can't wait!" I kind of knew Jack was already there because our different digital systems were starting to act up. I then read about the energy that scientists measure that surrounds the human body... the aura. It then explained how that could interfere with the electromagnetic workings of a computer. I was certain if ever I was to exude energy, it certainly would be just prior to hearing from him. I also figured his presence of Spirit energy might also affect electric or electronic equipment around our home just before a reading.

I was not surprised that the house alarm system that night voiced an error message, "Alarm not ready," when I tried to set it for the night. This time, the display case gave no error information and looked normal. It was just a single voiced error, but it worked fine as I tried it a second time. It began to be very clear that the alarm system was one of his easy go-to gadgets to mess with along with the thermostat, the phone, the television, and the computer. He had affected the alarm system before, each time with a different error, but always getting back to normal. And each error, whether the front window, the office window, or this general one, didn't repeat. At least he kept it interesting. At the same time, while I was in his office that same night, the remote phone screen and printer control screen both lit up from sleep mode for no reason. These were the same unexplainable events that had happened before.

The next morning, when Gail and I were getting ready to Zoom, both of our computers were having problems. Mine said *internet connection unstable*. Hers, several hundred miles away, wouldn't connect either right before, so she went to her tablet. I used my phone and we made it work. Somehow, Jack was affecting us both at the same time, and our computers were both connected and functioning fine the instant the reading was done. My energy was very high at the end of the reading, but the computer was normal. That made me point at Jack.

It's so hard to wrap my head around how that can be... how his energy can be spread out to be in two places at once, or even more. For example, while I was having my first Zoom reading with Gail, my daughter was having her own "visit" from her dad that morning. It turned out that her Ring doorbell went off and there was no delivery, no one there or on her street. She checked her outside cameras as well (this continued to happen even in the new places she's lived with new Ring doorbells). And when I was having my red, pulsating blob experience, my other daughter was having red dots floating on her computer screen.

As I accept the limitation of my physical brain, I find I just need to accept the fact that I can't know how it is to be energetically spread out into the eternal Oneness of this universe. I can rely on a faith, a belief, and a trust that it just is, and that someday I'll understand when I transition back to Spirit. I graciously accept God or Source or Higher Spirit as being everywhere, so I assume our souls' fields of energy are, too. My personal conjecture is that our essence is a part of that universal Love the way Jack explained, like a ray of the sun or a drop of the ocean. I trust everyone has their own personal take on it all. The good news is, we get insight into some of what it's like without a body on the other side through successful medium readings and messages like I have had from Jack. When a loved one can communicate relatable images and communications to the medium, and that reader is open to receiving without an interfering ego mind, it's a match! As the sitter (the person getting the reading), my simple validations provide encouragement to the reader (medium) that she's on the right track. This time it was nine months after Jack's passing, and it all worked like a charm.

****

September 14, 2022

Gail: "Jack's telling me how proud he is of you. How you're expanding. He has so much love for you. He sees you cleaning... clearing the lanai and getting the handyman to clean up the dirty outside."

Me: "Yes."

Gail: "He saw you went to the *John Edwards Show* live, but he didn't make a connection there because he didn't need to... others needed it more. He saw you getting ready at home trying on all different outfits trying to wear something bright so John Edward could pick you out of the crowd. He's laughing... he says you two kept going around and around and around. Were you lost?"

Me: Laughing. "No. My daughter and I were in a parking garage going around and around, level after level, going up and then back down trying to find a spot."

Gail: "My son Jake in Spirit, said, 'Thank you for helping my mom.'"

Gail: "Jack says that your love story transcends all lifetimes. He says to you, 'Trust me... I'll help you put all the pieces together for the writing.' He's laughing about messing with the electronics.... He's with his dad who had the same name, had knee surgery, and played golf. He's also with his mom and Aunt Evelyn. He says he used to shoot pool and was a pool shark... confident but humble. A happy loving soul."

Me: "Yes, he played pool as a teenager and was quite good. Fun-loving guy. And his dad's name was his. His dad also loved golf, and he did have knee surgery!"

Gail: "You know, you are the love of his life... you had a beautiful life together. There is a teddy bear he once gave you for Valentine's Day that you might want to dig out for a warm hug at night. He said he always went above and beyond to make you feel special and loved.... and he tried to put other's needs above his. He's puffing out his chest now, so proud of his daughters, so proud of Daddy's little girls... strong women. The older one is strong, and the younger one is tough-skinned, too... tough on the outside. All his girls are able to support one another... Jack's family of four, with a strong foundation like an Egyptian pyramid."

I knew I had answered Gail more than just yeses. Since she was practicing with me, I wanted her to know how on-point she was, and how she was interpreting so well what was coming through. I made sure I didn't give up any new information, only the details of what she already shared. At the same time, it was so affirming and warmed my heart. For just a little while, once again, I felt Jack's presence right there with me and proving it. I couldn't be happier!

Gail: "He's saying about you and him, 'As for us, we managed to become equal in our lifetime of spiritual growth, in alignment.' He's reminding you of this evolution of souls."

Me: "Yes, we did. Can I ask a question of him? Is it objectionable that I use some of his ashes for memory jewelry for me and the girls?" Gail: "He says he loves the idea of a necklace to wear on your chest near your heart. He's laughing. He says, 'You could vacuum them up with the vacuum cleaner for all I care. I'm not the body,

182

anyway.' He's not bothered by using some ashes. As for your book, he says that who's supposed to hear the message will buy it."

I never mentioned necklaces, but that's what I had been wanting to give our daughters if they wanted them. I also hadn't asked about the book, but I had been wondering how I would be able to spread our wonderful discovery about consciousness continuing in the afterlife. He obviously knew my thoughts! I went on to dare to ask another question and hoped for interaction. I was invited to a seventieth birthday party of a neighbor, one from Jack's cigar smoking group. I knew Jack's cigars were special, expensive, and he joked were his prized possession. He couldn't enjoy them in his last few months, so there were still several there in his humidor. I remembered he had told me once that, after he died, when family and friends come to visit me and sit outside, to share his cigars with them to remember him and our good times. Now I was wondering if I should also give them away, like to our neighbor for his birthday.

Me: "Gail, I have another question. Do I give out some of his cigars to friends?"

Gail: "He's holding up one finger. Jack is saying, 'Give them each one. Save the cigars for those who come to visit.' Also, go to the hair salon to get your hair cut before the party... you don't need to color it."

Me: "I was just planning to cut my own hair!"

Gail: "He says, 'I feel your feet tingling, numb... it's your diet. Your blood sugar is fine.' He sees you reading tons of books. Laughing, he says, 'Just pick one already, woman!' As for grief and the brain, he says you're doing fantastic... growing. He saw you during a scary thunderstorm... you in the house and scared. He says, 'I was wrapping you in a circle of energy, holding you safe to comfort you, but your busy brain did not sense me... a lesson.' He's always surrounding you... be aware, know he's there whether you sense or feel him or not.

He says, 'Angels are real.' He's referring to a love letter he wrote to you. He says, 'This whole synergy of our big love is amazing... now with an agenda to share our love story with your voice for me.' You are his angel, and he is yours now. 'It's a two-way street for us two. This lifetime as equals in Spirit... two souls, all together, all consciousness together."

Gail: Getting a download from Jack and her son, Jake. "Jack wants you to know this from Jake about our soul. He is still in the spiritual realm... still... we all are... our Higher Self residing in the spiritual realm... a small piece of us goes in the body. Imagine a SIM card in the phone.

Spirit is like that card plugged into the physical body... carries everything that was and will be... inhabiting and animating here in a soul growth. Then the SIM card pops out, keeping all the learnings and reunites into the spiritual realm. We really aren't ever disconnected... we are always connected... still connected... even during our physical time. We're just physically attending our bodies when incarnated.

Jake said that as long as she is still Gail, he'll be Jake. When they're done, they'll go back to the Oneness. There was one last thing... Jack's tree. Does he have a Legacy Tree?"

Me: "Years ago, I gave him a little date nut palm tree for his birthday that he asked for and loved, and I noticed it needed trimming just last week. I had hired someone to do that, and we were talking yesterday about how majestic it was. It has grown over thirty feet since we planted it, and I had said that I wished Jack could see it now. What a great validation that he does!"

Gail: "He wants you to remember he loves you and is always around you."

Me: "Thank you so much. Knowing he is around has been so comforting. I can't tell you what a difference you have made in my life!"

****

Gail said in her reading that Jack referenced angels in a love letter he once wrote to me. A few years prior to his transition, I gave him a letter for his birthday telling him what I loved about him. He was really moved by it and had tears in his eyes. Remembering that, the following year, when he asked me what I wanted for my birthday that was coming up, I told him, "Just a letter from the heart," and smiled. This was what he wrote telling me he wanted to describe me over our entire lifetime together. It says so much about him.

Eulogy for Bobbi - 2012

The first time I saw her she took my breath away. She was the quintessential Polish beauty. She had it all, looks, intelligence, charm, you name it. I knew at that moment she was worth it. Worth the risk of rejection and embarrassment because she surely outclassed me. But being both bold and stupid, I approached her, and when I looked into her eyes, I could see all the way to Heaven. I knew then there must be a God, and that if he made anything more wonderful, he must have kept it for himself.

Someone told me a story years ago about how the Almighty, in an effort to restore grace and love to the world, had sent 1,100 angels down to Earth. Each angel was to recruit another

1,100 angels, and those 1,100 were to recruit 1,100 more, etc., until the entire world was enlightened. After knowing Bobbi for almost 45 years, I am convinced she was one of the 1,100. She treated everyone who came into her life, whether friend, acquaintance, family member or a simple passerby, with great care, concern, and dignity.

She was a teacher. But to say she taught and counseled children, their parents, and the school staff members for some 33 years would be an understatement.

She taught every person who ever came within earshot of her for her entire life. When I think of her as a teacher, I am reminded of the old Greek teacher/philosopher who asked his students to come to the edge of a cliff. They did not want to because they were afraid to fall off into the abyss of what they didn't know. But he kept coaxing them, telling them to trust him, and that everything would be all right if they just did what he asked.

Eventually, the story goes, they got the courage to come to the edge, and when they did... he pushed them, and they flew. That was the kind of teacher she was. Always looking for your best. Always asking you to go further... to reach higher.

As a professional Life Coach, she was always juggling a dozen or so clients at any one time, and usually only getting paid from one or two at the most. If it was up to her she would never charge anyone a dime to help them. Her friends called her the

Bobbi Lama. She had an enormous capacity for love... both giving and receiving. No person, no animal was ever alone when in her presence. Her grandchildren were her true joy in later life. Always concerned for their safety and constantly doting over them. She always tried to emulate her grandmother who showed her such great love when she was a child. Another angel, no doubt.

It became clear to me some time ago why I was on this planet. To look out for her. I was supposed to keep anyone from taking advantage of her naivety and good nature and to keep her from harm. A task that I willingly accepted. My reward was that I got to bask in the light of her love.

She asked me for a special gift on this her birthday. She asked me to tell her what I thought of her, in writing and in my own words. So here is what I think... Wow! I guess I was the lucky one!

****

Jack's letter disclosed how big and open his heart was and what a humble man he chose to be. He still does have a capacity to love with great passion, intensity, and dimension. He always saw the good in people and tried to keep life enjoyable. He wasn't a complainer, and he always tried to put others' needs way out ahead of his own. He was generous to everyone he knew, and he was well known for it. It is no wonder he is able to reach out and continue being such a strong communicator and such a powerful frequency of Love. I know his efforts to help me know he's not gone have required cleverness, creativity, and persistence, like the feather story. There have been other times things have fallen over, or dropped off shelves that can't be explained, and yet truly served to ease my mind as I grieved his absence. The items themselves always had relevance to our history, or a timeliness when they occurred, or a meaningfulness between us that lead me to interpret them as communications. Like the time I went to the Hallmark Store to get a birthday card on what was to be our fifty-fourth anniversary. As I went around a corner display, a card fell on the floor alongside of me. It was a Happy Anniversary to My Wife card with a beautiful message inside. My eyes filled with tears... the coincidence was too strong.

****

When I think of the one with the most meaning, I can't help but remember the funny stories of that old classroom dummy I described earlier that fell off the shelf of a closet one night after he passed. Back when I was a teacher, my classes were involved in an *Invent America Contest*, and we were creating a comedy skit that would involve a life-size "person." Rather than searching for a mannequin, I offered to just make it myself. The night that I originally started creating the dummy, I had spent hours cutting, sewing, and stuffing the life-sized body. I didn't have enough time to finish the head, so I just laid it on the living room floor behind two chairs, somewhat out of the way to work on the next day. That night, Jack came home late to find it in the dark on the floor, and he thought it was me. He was totally freaked out. He said I almost gave him heart failure.

There were times I would dress it up as Santa or a Halloween witch and put it in the window for fun. He said it was freaky, like the movie *Psycho*. And once, when he had been gone a lot, I dressed it up as him and sat it in his seat at the dining room table with a sticker on its chest that read, "Hello, my name is Uncle Daddy." Our daughters really laughed at that one, and when he came home much later that night he did, too. There was also the time when the dummy was on a foyer chair by our front door ready to go back with me to my classroom in the morning. That evening, we had a prowler in our yard and I called the police. After the officer checked it out, he came inside the front door to talk with me. Because I had told the dispatcher I was home alone, he was surprised to see what looked like a person out of the corner of his eye as he turned to leave. It was sitting right by the front door where he had just entered and hadn't seen it. He instantly grabbed for his gun, and it gave me a start. Once he saw it was a dummy, we both had a good laugh. Jack used to tell that story, embellishing it more and more every time to keep making it funnier. I guess that's why it makes sense as to why he would choose the dummy to push over. I'd just love to know how!

****

Late one evening, I heard another loud bang, but this time it was from inside the garage. When I opened the door to check it out, I found the giant laundry detergent jug lying on the floor in front of me. Thank goodness it wasn't very full, so it didn't crack open and splatter. It had been sitting squarely on the shelf by the washing machine where those jugs always sat, so, once again, it made no sense. Right then, I realized that I hadn't brought the car into the garage when I got home that afternoon. It was sitting in the driveway unlocked, and our neighborhood had been having a lot of car break-ins in the evenings over the past few months. I grabbed my keys, went outside, and pulled the car into the garage. The next morning, I got a text from my next-door neighbor with an attached video. It was a recording from his outside camera showing four hooded teens running through the neighborhood around 3:00 am going from driveway to driveway trying car doors parked outside. The police later said four cars had been stolen on our local streets that night, and personal items were taken from other unlocked cars. Mine would have been one of them if it weren't for that laundry detergent jug falling and getting my attention and bringing me out to the garage. I was so grateful for that attention-getting bang and have been so careful with that ever since. I just hope someday I can be as good of a guardian angel to help people as he has been for me.

"I am happy because I want nothing from anyone. I do not care about money. Decorations, titles, or distinctions mean nothing to me. I do not crave praise. I claim credit for nothing. A happy man is too satisfied with the present to dwell too much on the future."

-Albert Einstein

Chapter 11 – We Go On

So, here's what I've learned from just one year after Jack's passing:

† We go on. We are in an eternal experience of energy during which our consciousness continues. Jack has proven that to me. His Spirit has worked so hard, dedicated to reach me so that "our story" can be told. He has kept his promise to let me know when he got there, and exactly as he said he would. He absolutely is not gone.

† The flavor of his essence from the other side continues to permeate his messages exactly as I remember him in his physical body. The threads of his edgy humor, kind generosity, loving compassion, bold confidence, and selfless love can still be felt so strongly in his tone, his timing, and his cleverness. He hasn't lost the essence of "him." He's still the man I married, raised a family with, grew old with, and cared for throughout our fifty-four-year physical journey together.

✝ We are only physically separated. We are still connected by Love in the Divine dimension. He has convinced me that he is around me all the time whether I'm aware of his energy or not. His evidential messages have become so validated.

✝ He has truly supported me, at first with signs, then watching out for me, giving me comfort, and supplying all the evidence I'd need to validate "our" book. He's laid the groundwork so I would have a mission through which I can learn my life lessons as well as serve others. He has assured me that I have the strength to do it, and he's promised me he'd be there for me to help make that happen. I've witnessed his being with loved ones other than me and sometimes even simultaneously, like with both my daughters.

✝ It is clear to me that after passing, the Spirit is no longer functioning from his or her ego mind that accompanied the body. Motives of Spirit come through as selfless love and caring... a field of energy that is for the good of all. It is a Source, God, or Higher Power creative intelligence that is described from near-death experiencers as so inexplicably beautiful.

✝ I'm not afraid of transitioning over anymore. I find it hard to even use the word "dead" now. I know we shed the physical body, but our Spirit doesn't die. Our essence or soul just continues on. Just to be clear, I'm not in a hurry, because I'm so connected with my family and friends, and I want to experience all that I can while I'm here. My plan is to help others find peace, too. I'm simply no longer afraid "to die."

✝ Knowing what I know now, I can live life differently. I recognize that when we are in our physical form, very often our fears relate to survival which then motivate much of what we do. We avoid serious risks, amass belongings, work to stay in control, and so on. Living from love, however, allows for letting go, being authentic, sharing, and working to understand and respect all others. After all, we are all doing the best we can with what we think we know. Being in acceptance of that is what I am using as my compass now.

✝ I've learned to accept relationships as growth opportunities and appreciate the roles being played by all my loved ones as mutually beneficial. It's like we're in "Earth school" where we have a physical lifetime's worth of experiences. We grow and hopefully learn more kindness, generosity, understanding, and compassion through all our interactions. I'm still learning from Jack. Eternity should give us plenty of time to enjoy *being* that state of Love. Communications from our loved ones in the hereafter can take any form, but only if we are open to receive, accept, and trust. A quiet mind receives best. It also helps me to practice discerning between my own thoughts that I generate, as opposed to those that seem to arrive and interrupt my busy linear thoughts. I welcome and enjoy every interruption!

✝ I now know Spirit can take any form, be any age, and present in any way that the message is best delivered. I believe time is a construct of the physical world, and the energy of Spirit does not have to deal in any timed dimension.

✝ I have come to know that my skepticism about his signs was a simple, automatic response at first. I needed to process my doubts and questions about every unexplainable event before I began to trust this new connection. After all, when something appears broken, your responsible habit is to figure out why and then fix it. However, seeing how many times I needed to be blown away, I realize how resistant we are to any concept we've been trained to question. Once I recognized the synchronicities that created the relevance and meaning of the communications, it became easier to receive. Eventually I went from grief to relief, welcoming every contact that proved he was not gone.

✝ I realize that soul energy is expansive beyond my ability to fathom, witnessing Jack's ability to affect electronics in places hundreds of miles apart simultaneously. I know I'll not understand it until I'm on the other side.

✝ I believe that when I am on the other side, I will be able to have clarity on the effects of all I've done here while in the physical body, both good and bad. Jack's messages have made it clear you remember the past you have accumulated. He's shared it's all Love. He's encouraged me to believe it is only right now that it is beyond my imagination or ability to understand. I will when I get there. And since energy cannot be destroyed, it's eternal, so we're eternal. Again, I can't wrap my head around that, but it means to me that my life here must be just a blip in the infinite scheme of things. Looking at the difference Jack made while he was here, I would like to be a better person, too, to come from a place of love and acceptance, avoid living in the past or the future, and make a difference in the lives of others in the attempt to leave this place better for having been here. I'm hoping, with Jack's help, we will have shed light on the fact that consciousness continues. He certainly has done his part by dedicating his physical life to sharing our souls' mission, and then keeping his promise with an exuberance of communications from his afterlife... or I should say his continued life.

† I have learned how clever Spirit can be in order to connect with loved ones. Jack knew Yvonne and knew she would figure out it was him coming through in her reading. How he managed to create such an opportunity to connect Gail with a friend of Yvonne is beyond me. Then again, maybe he just saw an opportunity and exploited it. I have no idea, but I am impressed.

† I have discovered that, for the most part, when I want signs to feel connected to Jack, my urgency or neediness can block my receptivity. I believe that when my positive emotions elevate my frequency, and I am in a quiet mind, I can receive his messages more easily. Trying hard does not make it happen.

† I'm learning to look for the context of the event I question more than the possibility of it. The red blob pulsating on my screen is a slim technical

possibility, but the timing with the unexplained *ding dings* on my phone, coupled with the YouTube video from Dr. Gary Schwartz speaking on communications from our loved ones in the afterlife just gave it more meaning.

† Plus, I couldn't make it happen again even when I went back onto the site—and I have tried. I've learned that when you're ready to entertain the possibilities of an afterlife, then you will open up to it, and when you're not, you're just not. Because of the conversations Jack and I had about sending signs from the afterlife, it made it much easier to recognize his communications. He knew that energy could affect energy, and his promise was set in my memory. He messed with the thermostat from the other side within the first few days, and it made me pay attention, or I would have never made the connection. From that point on, I gradually became more and more open and receptive.

† What I've learned is how different life can be when you have peace in your heart, and I wouldn't have felt that if Jack weren't such a determined and powerful communicator. My gratitude translates to a joy I didn't believe was ever possible again.

✝ I'm the first to admit what I don't know, but what I do know now is that we go on, and love is forever.

****

My wishes for you are simple:

✝ My biggest wish is that you are willing to open your mind to the possible concept that we don't die... that our consciousness is an eternal energy. It's actually exciting to discover that, don't you think? Our deceased loved ones are only "crossed over" and are right around you. How comforting is that?

✝ I hope you make plans for connecting with your loved ones from the hereafter before they transition to the other side. Let's face it, after they cross over, your skepticism is natural, and we need all the validating evidence we can get. Pick a sign or two, or a category and think in terms of energy. Jack told me he'd try to affect the thermostat, and it made sense. Best of all... it worked!

✝ Stay aware of those signs or events that are too hard to explain or "feel" unusual by paying attention to the accompanying circumstances. Notice what was going on in your thoughts right before your distracting sign, and don't be surprised with the speed with which your needs or requests are answered.

† Be aware of the "arrival" of thoughts as they seem "sent" into your mind and different from your thoughts, your flow, your rational or emotional direction, or your mood. These interruptions may be Spirit's energy "popping in a thought" from the other side.

† Be careful of doubt. It has a way of growing and keeping you skeptical in between signs and can rob you of the comfort that your loved one is near. Let your own questioning process consider the whole picture and be your guide. You'll know when to trust.

† Be appreciative of any sign, and open to the huge range of possibilities. The more I have read of other people's experiences, the more possibilities I can hope for even after the enormous variety of signs I've been so fortunate enough to receive in only our first year of our new connection.

† Use gratitude and love to raise your energy to help you connect with their lighter energy from the other side. I was just hearing in my head (from Jack?) the words from the song *Get Closer* by Seals

and Croft: "Darlin' if you want me to be closer to you, get closer to me." I think he just reminded me to say that staying lighter will reward you with that beautiful contentment of our shared, eternal field of Oneness. Talk to your loved ones with the trust they would love to hear back from you. If you were crossed over, wouldn't you want to know if those you left behind were comforted by you now from the other side? Wouldn't it please you to know that your efforts created a synchronicity to get their attention? They would like to know you received and believed your communications, I'm sure. I also assume those who I love and have passed on are around me, infused in my overall space, not just "over" me or "up there." Try to accept their presence as connected near you, with you, and deeply into your own soul's loving energy field (my ear just started ringing to affirm this).

✝ Practice relaxing your busy mind. Lord knows it isn't easy. Quieting the very part of us that is built-in to serve our ego and survival will feel unnatural, but it's worth it. Let's face it, being preoccupied will limit our awareness, but, then again, no thought is not possible. Find meditations that work for you, ones that help you simply be present. Become aware of your breath, the breeze, the sounds around you in a receiving kind of way. Softly dismiss judgment and interpretations to be just in acceptance of being part of the universal loving Oneness. Getting into observer mode to be aware and in the moment will reduce the noise in your head and open you up to receive even more.

† And lastly (knowing Jack is still giving me strength, direction, and a loving "push") *our* overall wish is that you feel the connection with your loved ones, so you never have to feel separated again.

Epilogue

*A*s I was getting ready for one more medium reading with Gail, I found a scribbled note of something I had meant to include in the book and hadn't. Jack always used to say that it was the imperfections that made everything and everyone perfect. That their uniqueness is what makes them special, interesting, and enjoyable. Not thirty minutes later during the reading, I asked Gail if Jack thought I said everything I needed to say in *our* book. I asked if I left anything out.

Gail got quiet and then answered, "I'm hearing him say, 'Perfectly imperfect.' Did I understand this?" I got the chills, explained why he said that, and then she got the chills.

I also remembered when Gail told me Jack said, "Send my love." I wasn't sure who it was to be sent to... me? Our daughters? Our family, friends, and neighbors? It was when we were talking about his support for me writing this book. He reminded me that those who needed comfort and reassurance that their loved ones are still near would get it. At that given moment, my outdoor lights flickered a few times and then were fine. How he managed to "answer me" with such perfect timing, I have no clue... just trust. And since his authentic love is so expansive and passionate now, I believe *his love* is for all of us, including you, my reader.

And lastly, I personally hope that this combined lifetime effort of ours can help give comfort to others who feel "separated" from their transitioned loved ones. Ours was a spiritual journey knitted together with a love that was a powerful soul connection. This double-soul plan for our eventual physical separation would help us manifest the knowing that our consciousness came before, during, and after that short physical experience. I have felt the support of his compassionate energy throughout the telling of our story, knowing he, too, is trying to show communication is possible from the other side. I can see now, at the end of my life, that our souls were joined together for a bigger purpose. I feel like we are straddling our two frequencies to complete this message, with him sending, and with me receiving to show this Loving Oneness can give us all comfort and peace.

About the Author

Bobbi was a teacher for twenty years and then a school counselor for fourteen. She also has a teaching certification for mathematics and for substance abuse counseling. She had her own business as a Certified Life Coach for ten years after retiring and then as a Certified Clinical Hypnotherapist for five. She is a Reiki Master, has recorded her own relaxation and healing meditations, and authored a book on counseling middle schoolers (*Behind the Counselor's Door: Solutions to the Most Common Middle Schooler's Problems*). Once her husband Jack needed daily care, she took that on exclusively. She now writes for her blog called *Tales from the Bobbi Lama*.

She and Jack met in college in 1967 and were married in 1969. They had two daughters and now have six grandchildren. Bobbi's passion has been to help people find peace and joy, so, after Jack passed, she decided to continue to give hope and comfort to others by sharing their phenomenal connection across the veil.

For questions or updates, go to her website:
www.bobbirise.com.